NEW LIFE FOR YOUR SUNDAY SCHOOL

Other Books by the Author

THE DYNAMICS OF CHRISTIAN EDUCATION
TWO SEASONS: ADVENT AND LENT
(WITH KENDIG BRUBAKER CULLY)
CHILDREN IN THE CHURCH
IMPARTING THE WORD: THE BIBLE IN CHRISTIAN EDUCATION
AN INTRODUCTORY THEOLOGICAL WORDBOOK
(WITH KENDIG BRUBAKER CULLY)
WAYS TO TEACH CHILDREN
CHRISTIAN WORSHIP AND CHURCH EDUCATION
CHANGE, CONFLICT, AND SELF-DETERMINATION

NEW LIFE FOR YOUR SUNDAY SCHOOL

Iris V. Cully

HAWTHORN BOOKS, INC.
W. Clement Stone, *Publisher*
NEW YORK

NEW LIFE FOR YOUR SUNDAY SCHOOL

 All inquiries should be addressed to Hawthorn Books, Inc., 260 Madison Avenue, New York, New York 10016. This book was manufactured in the United States of America and published simultaneously in Canada by Prentice-Hall of Canada, Limited, 1870 Birchmount Road, Scarborough, Ontario.

Library of Congress Catalog Card Number: 75-28684
ISBN: 0-8015-5366-0
1 2 3 4 5 6 7 8 9 10

Contents

Preface

Most Protestants go by the formula that Sunday School equals religious education, and Catholics feel that parochial school, with or without Confraternity of Christian Doctrine (CCD), equals religious education. When a special form of teaching has been around a long time, we tend to assume it will continue. Even when there are obvious signs that something is wrong—a decrease in the number of pupils, a high teacher turnover, or reduced funds—we still hope that a little tinkering here and there will make things right again.

Some churches opt for new forms. A family evening or afternoon classes become popular. Weekends for young people replace Sunday evening groups. Morning coffee supplements the adult class. These may work or they may not. The search for new forms in itself indicates concern both for the task and the people involved. Everyone responds with renewed interest. Later, this too will flag. There are fundamental factors which do not depend on time, place, or method. These are basic to any improvement.

People are learning through whatever goes on within a congregation. A church's activities reach out into the community as people are invited successively to bazaars, suppers, lectures, or revivals. How does your community see the church? Is there a balance among fellowship, money-raising events, and those events which proclaim the gospel more directly? Activities may say one thing to adults but something else to children. For example, a parent's involvement in activities gives the adult an assurance of acting as a responsible church member, but children in the family may feel that the church has taken away a parent! This doesn't happen where members share the work, but it is something to watch.

Every congregation sees, in addition, a specific teaching task. This is rooted in the ancient Jewish practice, described in Scripture as teaching the Law to the children and introducing them to God's wonderful action in saving his people. It is indicated by the story of Jesus calling the children to him and of the practice by the first Christians of meeting in homes for prayer, scripture reading, and the breaking of bread. That is why we set aside a special time for teaching. This book is dedicated to the improvement of the time. Read it alone or in a group. Pick up suggested activities. Do further reading. It will not *tell* you how, but it will *show* you how you can improve your Sunday School.

NEW LIFE FOR YOUR SUNDAY SCHOOL

1
Why Do You Have a Sunday School Anyway?

A church with an active teaching program has specific characteristics: high pupil attendance, low teacher turnover, interested parents and other adults. These churches have one thing in common, *a specific goal with which all, including the minister, agree.*

The *Bible* could be central: We want pupils to learn the content of the Bible and be able to live by it.

Commitment might be the goal: Our purpose is to bring pupils to an experience of Christ so that they will commit their lives to him.

Belief could be the keynote: We want our pupils to be able to affirm the triune faith in such a way that they can know God and tell others of their belief.

Church could be the clue: We want our pupils to reach a point at which they will affirm their Christian faith in terms of loyalty to God's church and find service and orientation from its sacraments and fellowship.

A *way of life* could be the aim: We want pupils to know what it means to live as a Christian and to conduct their lives according to the teachings of Christ.

You will say that all of these are part of the goal. Of course; but one central point must stand clearly in view. The rest is descriptive.

On the other hand are congregations in which several groups of people see the goal differently. The minister hopes for faithful members; parents want their children to learn the Bible (or the faith); teachers want to get across a lesson this Sunday; the governing board wants to know that many people are being served. Do you see what I mean? Each person or group has a specific goal (or is it a hope?); the overall picture is diffuse. The elements are scattered and there is no concerted effort at a unified purpose. In fact, some may seem to be at cross-purposes and criticism could set in. Parents say, "I want my child to learn the Bible," and teachers reply, "It's all I can do to get through a Sunday morning." The minister says, "We need more committee members," and the board says, "We can't possibly give the Sunday School as much money as it wants." Nobody is really getting together with anyone else. The whole enterprise is weakened.

Describe Your Goal

In addition to being specific, *the goal must be one which is not being accomplished elsewhere*. For example, take the goal of Christian living. The Gospel is expressed in lives, but some of the qualities that we call Christian are really human, decent ways of acting, which any person should be expected to evidence. In order to function harmoniously, a society requires people trained to show kindness, honesty, and respect for the rights of others in personal relationships and through public responsibilities. All religions teach this. People do not need to get up on Sunday morning to learn how to be human. This presses us to examine exactly what is distinctive to the Christian life. What, if anything, makes the Christian person different from the good person who is a nonbeliever. Perhaps it is motivation—feeling close to God, being indwelt by the Holy Spirit, feeling a nearness to Christ. It could be a life of witness, showing the fruits of the Spirit. We speak of the spirit in which something is done, of an attitude of self-giving or of joy in well-doing. However you describe it, there must be some plus to the term *Christian living* that will make it a goal with power. It must be distinctive.

A third characteristic of a useful goal is that it is stated in such a way that the results can be described and recognized. Go back to the central goals mentioned at the beginning of the chapter. Any one could be a focus. But you can't expect pupils, teachers, parents, minister, and congregation to work together to fulfill goals until they have some common way of describing what they are looking for when they state the goal. You don't want a narrow description—you are working with people, not paper dolls. God works in his own mysterious ways, and not every Christian shows forth the new life in exactly the same way as others. Each brings a whole personhood to God with distinctive ways of being and acting. You surely have some ideas of what a mature Christian is like, and it is important to share your ideas with others involved in the nurture of young Christians (or new ones).

For example, how do you know that a person is committed to Christ? No one disputes another's affirmation. We rejoice in it! Is it shown in a look, a glow, a tone of voice? Is it spoken? Specific actions? Or look at that goal about the centrality of the Bible. You don't simply mean a knowledge of the content of the Bible. One solid school course can do more in that direction than twelve years of Sunday School, but it would be done differently. It would be an intellectual understanding of the text and its background. What you want for young believers is an understanding of the Bible as the Word of God, and there must be ways in which you can describe the results of this kind of biblical teaching. Is it that one learns sentences and passages which come to mind at special times of joy or pain, hope or despair to strengthen faith? Is it that the knowledge of One Life makes him the companion to other lives? Is it learning the Lord's commands in such a way that this is shown in joyful obedience? (This person can be trusted because the Law of God is important in this life.) Is it the indwelling assurance of forgiveness that makes a person confident and always ready to extend forgiveness to others?

It must also be remembered that the expression of the goal differs with the time of life. Childhood is one of the times that God has given, and some of its qualities should be carried through life ("You must become as children.") A child will show relationship to God in a childlike way; the teenager will show it in an adolescent way. Adults will vary according to their time of life. We must also expect that the human relationships of life will have an effect. Those who have little experience of forgiveness find it difficult either to accept forgiveness or extend it to another. Those who have not known just commands kindly given cannot have the psalmist's experience of finding delight in the Law of the Lord. We do not describe goals in order to judge people, but they help us to know what we really want to do, and this is the first step toward improvement.

So much for description. Now to the steps by which you set about improving the goals. Allow yourselves plenty of time. This isn't to be done in an hour or two. It may take months. You may become so interested that you will spend a year on the work.

Who Determines Goals?

First find out where you are as a congregation. The minister will quickly and eagerly give you goals. Most clergy like to write, to give their ideas, and really want to see things done. However, don't spread those ideas around at first. If you do, people would simply be responding to the minister's goals. Instead, ask that these ideas be shared at a general meeting.

Suggest that the governing board spend a meeting or part of one discussing what they think is (are) or should be the goal(s) of the Sunday School. They may be astonished at the variety of opinions. Write down all ideas. Finally, arrange these into categories. Remember it is more important to discover how many goals there are at this stage than to try to reach some quick agreement. There will be time for that later.

Ask the religious education committee to spend a meeting on the same subject. They of all people should know what the goals are, but you don't want them to feel embarrassed if they do not agree. Many churches have never really tackled the question, and your people should feel good that they are going at it constructively. You may approach the subject in the same manner as with the governing board. Ask each person present to list goals, leaving the page unsigned. Collect these and redistribute so that each person reads another's paper. Write the main points on the chalkboard.

Discussion will develop. This group may also discover such diversity as to need time to develop a consensus before being ready to clarify their goals.

Teachers are the people closest to the need for goal setting because their work is to try to fulfill the goals. How seldom we give teachers this opportunity! Each one is handed a course book which defines the goal and purpose for each unit and session. Few readers see much relationship between these lofty statements and the sheer work of the Sunday morning class. So, for an evening, forget the books. Ask each teacher to state a personal understanding of what he or she hopes with God's help will happen after children have been in Sunday School for ten to twelve years. Then talk about these hopes. Here are people who should know, like, and trust each other because they are working on a common enterprise with the same children in the same place. As a matter of fact, in a large Sunday School they may seldom see each other, but that is another story. (See chapter 3.) This should be the most informal of all the meetings on the subject of goals and should have the most give-and-take among participants. They may not agree with each other any more than has another group, but they will surely realize the seriousness of the quest. Each teacher usually works with a pupil for only a year. This makes it important that each be assured of being part of a process of Christian nurture, building on what a previous teacher has done and trusting what others will do.

Parents are the first teachers of religion. Yet, if you were to ask what they want the church to do for their children, you might get general answers. Even a specific response like "I want my child to know the Bible" leaves a lot unsaid. Where do you begin when you want to know what parents are *really* thinking? Teachers who have a habit of calling on the parents of students might ask the question informally. If you are apt to meet them on the street or at the market you could take a casual approach. "By the way, we teachers have been asking ourselves what we hope will happen when children attend Sunday School. What do you think about it?"

Parents' meetings don't often attract a large attendance, but they do provide a discussion group. However, only actively interested people are going to think seriously about the subject anyway; so you might try planning such a meeting. A questionnaire sent home by mail (with a return envelope) might work if you make it easy to answer. Consider sending something like the following:

> Dear Mr. and Mrs. Jones:
>
> We know you believe that the Sunday School is important because you send your children. We also believe that the Sunday School is vital for Christian growth. We want to have a better Sunday School. Would you help us?
>
> Please write down what you think the Sunday School should accomplish. Just a few sentences will be fine, but write more if you wish. Be specific if you can, but give broader goals if you wish. Feel free to leave the letter unsigned.
>
> Please try to find the time to do this for us. Thank you.
>
> Sincerely,
>
> John and Jane Doe
> Bobby's teachers

Important: Be sure you report to the parents a summary of their ideas and that you share with them the goals that are later adopted.

Another idea is to list a number of concrete goals—say from five to ten—and leave a few blank lines for additions. Directions at the top of the sheet would read:

> To help us do a better planning job for your children, please tell us what you think should be our goals. Number the following in the order of your preference. Don't bother to include those you do not think are useful. Add any ideas of your own.

Some people will check a list who would never write a paragraph.

There is one more group who might like to be invited to share in goals: the whole congregation. You could give them the same checklist that you gave to parents. This could be the basis for a coffee hour, adult discussion group topic, a church supper, or a special emphasis evening on Christian education. You choose the occasion; then choose the method of presentation. Several have already been mentioned such as the use of a checklist, writing a descriptive paragraph, jotting ideas on a chalkboard, or asking people to volunteer ideas without comment.

This does not mean that in order to adequately set goals you must involve all these groups. Sometimes it will not be possible; sometimes it will not be wise. A large parish will need to poll more groups than will a small congregation where the same people belong to several groups. You should, however, eventually have something concrete to share with the whole congregation. Think how much this would do for the Christian education of all adults!

Putting It All Together

You aren't quite at the end. At some point you will need to narrow down the areas and focus the specific goals. You must decide how best to do this. It could be through a representative group of parents, teachers, board members, and representatives from the congregation. It could become the responsibility of the religious education committee, or if you do not have one, the governing board.

Remember what was said earlier about the way Christian life is shown differently at different ages. Here is where parents and teachers have a specific contribution. They need to get together in groups and represent the children they know best. Translate the goal into learning, behavior, and action for preschool children, for elementary children, for junior high and high school young people. Adolescents need to be involved in the goal setting for themselves and even, if they have time, in the setting of overall goals. Then each adult might be invited to think about how his or her life would be personally affected by such goals.

Now you have something concrete for everyone. Let's take a look.

1. A few briefly written, guiding statements about goals
2. One or more goals
3. Several statements describing each goal
4. The breakdown into age-group terms

You will say that every curriculum has such goals stated in its early pages. There will probably be an overall statement and goals outlined for each course. There will be a purpose described at the beginning of each unit and perhaps one for each session. Why not leave it at that?

For one reason, although teachers may read these statements, they rarely take them personally. Most people (including parents unless they are also teachers) do not read them at all. More important, they are written for large and small churches, in city and country all across the land. They represent the hopes of the editors, writers, and denominational officials more closely than the actualities of your situation. It cannot be otherwise. You will have to make a set of goals your own, or they won't really become operative. After you have taken the time and trouble to do this, you will be ready to look at your denominational or curricular goals. They become another factor in your description of goals.

They may give you ideas or a new way of stating thoughts. You can accept them because you see them in the perspective of your own self-understanding of what it is to be a Christian. You will better understand the process by which these people set about looking at goals and writing curriculum. You will understand the words they used. The abstract quality so often noticeable in overall statements will become enriched with the experience that you can put into them. You may modify these goals, rewrite them, or appropriate them. They become part of *your* total statement.

The children in your parish are your responsibility before God; so are the young people and adults. Parents, teachers, committee members, and all other adults are responsible for the continuing Christian nurture of one another. Setting goals is only the beginning of the task, the first step in the improvement of your Sunday School.

Don't be in a hurry. You could spend a month, three months, or a whole year on the job. You might do it in the spring or summer as preparation for a new year or it might become a continuing task. It could be a one-month emphasis involving everyone in a special work. It could be done slowly and quietly. You know your people. Only you can set the pattern of the way it will be done.

Do it with prayer. Meditate thoughtfully on Scripture. And God will reward your sincere efforts to know his purposes in your goals.

Summary

Improving the Sunday School begins with having a few specific goals for which there is wide agreement. To determine these:

1. Gather small groups having specific responsibilities: the governing board, religious education committee, teachers, parents, young people, the congregation.
2. With these varied answers in hand, work again with each group, then with an overall or representative group to achieve a concrete set of goals.
3. Gather people who know each age-group in the Sunday School so that they can write a description of the goals in terms of each developmental stage.
4. Choose some way of making the results widely known: letter, church bulletin, a special event.

Points to remember.

1. You may not wish to involve every group in the church. Which could be most helpful?
2. Vary the methods used. Do you need brief answers or long ones? Is it better to ask for oral or written replies?
3. Do you want to give a general invitation to people to participate in this work or would it be better to select people?
4. How do you mesh your goals with the curricular or denominational statement of goals?
5. What timetable will you set for the work?

What are you going to do with these goals now that you have them?

2
Teachers—How to Get Them

One mark of the successful Sunday School is its teachers. (I know pupils are important, but I will discuss them in a later chapter). If you are a new or small congregation, few people may be available to teach. If you are a tired parish that has gone along on past momentum for years, it may have become a habit for people who start teaching to give up quickly. There is said to be a 25 percent turnover every year. Many teachers remain on the job less than two years. A minister, superintendent, or religious education committee could spend a lot of time just looking for replacements—to say nothing of trying to find substitutes for the absentee teachers who may or may not phone before not appearing Sunday morning. Sometimes there is a good reason. Children do wake up on Sunday morning with a fever, and a parent has to stay home.

Is Sunday School Necessary?

What will you do if you come to a point where nobody seems to care? Believe it or not, some have tried the most drastic solution of all: dropping the Sunday School. Before you gasp in shock, remember that the church has kept strong many years through the participation of believers in their common worship (see chapter 10). Scripture is heard and the Word is preached. Prayer is learned best by praying. Hymns tell about the common Christian experiences. The offertory is the self-giving of the worshippers. There is surely no better way to deepen your love of God, strengthen commitment, and understand what it means to be a Christian.

Nevertheless, my guess is that to disband the Sunday School would be a temporary situation. Either you would find a means of education to replace it, or everyone would miss the Sunday School and begin to ask how to revive it. Volunteers would appear, and soon you would be off to a new start. While church members take their children to the morning service, the Sunday School is the only way to reach children whose parents are not themselves interested in church but who want some religious education for their children. The possible loss of the Sunday School might encourage people to think about why they had one in the first place. This could increase its importance in the mind of everyone.

Why do people volunteer to teach? Some do because they think there ought to be a Sunday School, or they think their children ought to go to Sunday School. Someone ought to teach and they are somewhat willing. Important as these responses are in bringing forth potential teachers, they are hardly the expression of a deeply felt need for Christian nurture. Here is where careful goals can sustain the work.

If you are starting from scratch, you will not want many teachers, even if by some strange coincidence there is a rush of volunteers. You will need only a few carefully selected ones. This is a time to set standards—when you are at the very beginning (or at the bottom, if having no teachers seemed to be a catastrophe). The reason you need only a few is because a starter program calls for an ungraded school.

If this sounds like the oldest educational system you know about—the one-room country schoolhouse—you may realize that it is also the newest idea to come upon the scene. It is not the "huddle" system that you may remember from earlier Sunday School years when a small circle of children gathered around each teacher in a large room, sometimes separated from the sight of other classes by temporary partitions which doubled as bulletin boards.

The new way is to treat a large group as a single teaching unit engaged in individual learning and forming groups to accomplish specific tasks. Those of you who use the uniform lessons will immediately see the possibilities. The basic Scripture passage is read and the story told to the whole group, which may include several grades. Then three or four teachers, as available, can work with small groups exploring the story in various ways: making a poster, dramatizing a scene, writing an explanation, answering a quiz, or responding to an illustration. The ideas are already in the teaching guides you use. In this setup, you make all the methods available at once, permitting pupils to make choices. They move from one learning center to another, completing the work at one before changing to the next area. Interest rather than age determines the choice.

Note that this plan calls for one lead teacher or better still a team for mutual support. Try a husband-wife, mother-daughter, or two-friend team. No active church is so poor in human resources as to be unable to find two such people and to supplement them with helping teachers. The latter could sign up for a definite period such as one unit of study. Some will prefer to volunteer their particular abilities in music, drama, story telling, biblical understanding, or the use of audiovisual materials. Just think of the savings in the continuous use of materials instead of duplications for many small classes. Most important, this kind of setting is a training ground for new teachers. When your group is large enough to break into smaller units, you may find your team willing to split and form new teaching teams. Perhaps two helpers will decide to become a team.

A Place for Preschoolers

A basic group could be very large, but you may wish at some point to separate the preschoolers. By now you may be enjoying the ungraded form so much that you will not change no matter how many teachers volunteered. To have people waiting to teach makes teaching a sought-after job. How often do you see that happen? If there are few children in your church, the ungraded group may seem like a large family in which the youngest receive special attention and being alone might work to their disadvantage. Preschoolers, however, have special needs. They can't read; so some of the activities of the larger group are closed to them. When preschoolers are alone they can change activities quickly (their interest span is brief), and they can be given more opportunities to use physical activity in their learning.

This means increasing the number of teachers, but this is the easiest group for which to find helpers. People balk at teaching older children because they feel uncertain of the ability to answer questions boys and girls ask. They are less hesitant to deal with the developing religious experience of the preschooler. Perhaps they do not realize that little children can ask big questions. However, be glad for the people who can respond to little children for this is the time when basic attitudes are developing. The child who feels welcomed and happy in the church can feel assured that God is love.

Infants need a place for themselves. Few parents can sit each Sunday beside a small child and not convey some sense of anxiety lest the child not behave as some adults in the congregation might wish. The "crying room" is no help because, while it keeps sounds from the rest of the congregation, one restless child can affect others. Mothers, wishing to hear the service, strain to be comforting to the child while feeling deprived themselves. It is better to have several motherly persons who during Sunday School, the church service, or both will take turns staying with the under-twos, conveying a warm, quiet sense of love to those in crib or playpen.

Very large Sunday Schools separate the two-year-old children but they are such stolid little creatures when by themselves that it is almost a kindness to put them with the livelier threes from whom they learn how to play and to listen and in other ways participate with other children. Don't expect much conformity. They are not ready to come into a story circle simply because someone says it is story time.

The subject is the recruitment of teachers, and we seem to be talking about conducting the Sunday session. However, this is why you are recruiting; so you have to define the task before you can ask people to teach. So far several things have been said about how to attract teachers:

1. Drop the Sunday School temporarily and go without teachers. The service of worship becomes the teaching vehicle.
2. Recruit one or two people who will organize and plan an ungraded school.
3. Add helpers with special skills to sign up for a unit, a year, or a special project.
4. Separate into age-groups and increase the number of teachers accordingly.

This gradual increase permits you to make clear the goals of the Sunday School to each new teacher so that those who take on teaching responsibilities really know what they are committed to.

Include Young People

Young people should not be forgotten. Junior highs would have no trouble at all fitting into an ungraded room because they enjoy being helpful and will learn from assisting younger children. They feel important because they are older and have special skills. They will engage in activities that they would otherwise scorn as babyish and will learn through their participation as helpers. If it seems that they are ready for a kind of thinking that they cannot get in a class with younger children and if you have a person or team skilled to work with junior high students, it might be useful to find a place for them to meet alone. But if they are making an important contribution to the mixing of the larger group, find some other time for meeting their concerns.

Another point to remember is that in restricting the Sunday School to Sunday morning, we are restricting the possibilities for recruiting teachers. Those who have raised children and taught Sunday School at the same time appreciate the kind of organization necessary at home so that everything meshes from Saturday evening through Sunday morning. Some of the happiest junior high teaching has been done by a person or persons with young children or no children who thoroughly enjoyed the unique perspective brought into their lives by a weekly contact with boys and girls at this alert and questioning age. When recruiting, realize that sometimes people are challenged by a situation so different from the usual as to be a stimulating change.

What is said about junior high students goes equally well for the high school young people. Maybe Sunday morning is not the time for them to meet, although it might be a good time if there are adequate space for the kind of meeting they need and skilled persons available to teach. Frequently, young people are helping to teach children and are learning through this experience. Need it be said that Sunday School is not a substitute for attending morning worship?

The real recruitment problem comes in finding persons who understand the joys and problems of adolescents in their Christian development and whose own faith can be an inspiration to young people. Such adult leaders need flexibility and skill and must be able to accept disagreement and opposition with graciousness. Don't assume this to be a minister's job—even that of a young minister. The experience might make both minister and young people feel uncomfortable with each other for a long time afterwards. The ability to minister to a whole congregation does not convey special skills for working with a particular age-group. So always be on the lookout for people who can do this. In smaller communities, it might be wise to make such persons available to all the churches through some shared activities for junior high and high school students.

Recruitment for adult classes is part of a Sunday School's improvement, but there are so many possibilities that a separate chapter has been reserved (see chapter 9).

Finding Teachers

The gradual expansion of the number of persons needed to teach has been described, but an important word has not been said: Who finds these people and where?

You find them in your own congregation. Where else? You begin with some dramatic action which indicates the seriousness of the need. You surround each responsible teacher with helpers and resource people. There is still no substitute for the personal invitation. You are a salesperson, and you are also appealing to the conscience of a fellow church member. Only a person already involved in responsibility dare ask another. Be careful of two situations.

There is a saying that if you want work done, ask someone who is already active. Not necessarily so! Some persons seem unable to say no and eventually find themselves dropping out and feeling guilty or becoming overwhelmed with work and half-doing some of it. Be sensitive to the needs of the persons you consider asking. Do not put burdens on people who really need to be shown how to get out from under too much work.

Instead, look for a few people with ability and some self-assurance whether or not they have had experience in teaching. The minister is not the only person who should be recruiting, although admittedly this is the one person likely to know everyone, especially new people. Somehow it is easier to turn down the clergy: they are professionals. It is more difficult to turn down a volunteer who has been teaching. What I am saying is that it is important to match the visitor to the person you hope will become a teacher.

Finally, recruiting is just the beginning. When a person says yes to your request to teach, you have taken on a responsibility to support this new teacher in any way necessary. The next chapter is all about that.

Summary

Steps for a committee to take when looking for teachers:

1. Decide how few people are needed to do an adequate job. (This isn't a one hour guessing game.) Your Sunday School may need reorganization.
2. With the parish list in hand, the religious education committee or a specially selected group of people should jot down names of those who have had a successful teaching experience. Recruiting begins with the choice of a few dedicated, qualified people. Add possible newcomers and people who work well with children or youth. Be sure you balance male, female, young, old people, as well as resource and substitute teachers. Recruit people whose gifts match the situation and who are not already overworked.
3. From the same list, select the names of people who will ask others to teach. The recruiter is important; find someone already at work who can appeal as a co-worker. Include yourselves. This may seem like double work but if it means that only five people have to be asked to teach instead of ten, you are ahead. Some people have a gift for making a request

look like a privilege. Choosing recruiters is as important as making a list of potential teachers.

4. Bring the new recruits together to ask what you can do to help them feel comfortable in their job.
5. Realize that recruitment is only the beginning.

3
Teachers—How to Keep Them

Recruiting teachers will be an endless job if you do not use the same amount of effort in keeping them. You can never improve your Sunday School if you are not developing a stable teaching group. A teacher spends the first year learning—simply beginning to feel that the class will survive a session. By the second year, there is a degree of confidence that enables a teacher to be flexible, accept wrongdoing from children without feeling personally threatened, encourage questions without feeling that there must be a correct answer, and try out new methods. There are real advantages in paying close attention to the needs of the first-year teacher.

The new teacher is not the only one lacking confidence. Parents wonder at constant turnover. Some children take it as a challenge. They have been known (horrible thought) to try to get rid of teachers. Finally, this constant turnover is one of the factors that weakens the Sunday School within the power structure of the church. Other people stay for years, move from one official position to another; know the ins-and-outs of what can or cannot be done. The Sunday School rarely rates high with the governing board and is at the bottom of the list when money is being handed out. The Sunday School treasury of earlier years was a bad alternative. Separating it from the church, in effect, made the children pay for their own education. Has enough been said to indicate the importance of the task?

Strengthening Teachers

The first step should be easy but is too often neglected: the simple matter of morale. Somebody, probably the director or coordinator of Christian education or the superintendent, should be responsible for seeing that all teachers, especially new ones, are given constant encouragement. The basic need for reassurance can be met almost without cost. Somebody should be available to greet each teacher on arrival Sunday morning with a voice and manner which convey "I'm glad you're here and it is going to be a wonderful session." Maybe we should all say: "This is the day which the Lord has made. We will rejoice and be glad in it!" What this does is to send the teacher to class with confidence.

This gets through to the children, and they are more likely to respond positively. The greeting has another purpose: It gives the teacher an opportunity to express feelings. Maybe there wasn't quite enough time to prepare, and the teacher feels anxious. Maybe everything went wrong at breakfast, and the mood hasn't shaken off. This calls for special reassurance and an offer to stand by or look into the room during the session.

Teachers need further reassurance at the end of a session. Try to see each before leaving. "How did it go?" "Did you have the supplies you needed?" "What can I do for you for next week?" If you are in a hurry or the teacher is and especially if some things were left unsaid, be sure to phone the teacher that afternoon or evening. Listen to feelings while they are strong and deal with them.

Some schools are fortunate enough to have a church school office in which records, supplies, and curricular materials are readily available. This makes it necessary for the teacher to visit the room once during the session. Make this an attractive place where someone is always ready to be helpful. You might even have coffee available to invite a relaxing moment before or after the session.

Another important factor in morale is recognition by the congregation. Sunday School teaching can be the loneliest job in the church. In the most elaborate building, teachers and children are often segregated from the rest of the congregation. There are several ways of overcoming this. In the fall, a recognition and dedication service for teachers can be incorporated into morning worship. Please include a pledge by the whole congregation to support teachers with prayer, work, and money. Plan a coffee hour or reception after church at which teachers are the guests of honor and the governing board is highly visible introducing people to the teachers.

At the end of the year, arrange a time when everyone can visit classrooms and see work done. This might be on Sunday morning, or it could be a church family supper. Consider also a closing recognition dinner as a gift for teachers and their spouses (they help too). Be sure that members of the governing board are present. In a large church, the senior minister's presence is also importnat.

Paying for Education

The second step is providing adequate money for the Sunday School. Every church has a budget, and the proportion given to each sector indicates to everyone the importance with which the program is held. Sunday Schools are notoriously low on the list when funds are apportioned. Why? Usually they are not adequately represented on the finance or budget committee. Young parents, children, and newcomers who are teachers must have friends and representation in the right places. Bring stalwarts into the Sunday School as resource people. When the juniors are studying a unit on the church, ask a well-informed member to tell the children how the congregational structure works or brief the teachers in preparation for the unit.

Use the special skills of people. This kind of mutual acquaintance is important to establish interest in the Sunday School. Money, work, and concern will provide the kind of setting which says to teachers and children, "What goes on here is important and we are with you all the way."

For example, a cheerful room is a good beginning; it must be clean, attractively painted, with usable equipment, sufficient resources, needed supplies, and with no one else's junk around. One day I went to a very lovely church for a teacher-training conference. It was a Saturday morning, and as they listed the problems they wanted to discuss that day, the subject of rooms came up. "My room is a mess," one said. "Mine is filled with things from a weekday group," said another. They were not angry; they seemed resigned, as if this situation was to be expected. It was, as I have said, a lovely building. We were meeting in a comfortably furnished sitting room.

I suggested, "Let's go see your rooms." The response was

immediate. Everyone jumped up and a tour began. Up to this time, they had hardly noticed each other's rooms and not realized that this was a common problem. The minister, concerned enough to call the conference and be present for it, had not realized that the room situation was a real irritation to the teachers.

The reasons for the complaints soon became clear: Rooms were bare of decoration; furniture was uncomfortable and outdated; there was no space for books. At least two of the teachers used rooms which were hardly changed from their weekday use. It had never occurred to anyone that all the groups using a room might get together to figure out how each could use it without inconveniencing the other.

The needs were not expensive. There were lots of bulletin boards, but these were clumsily constructed and set in the wrong places. Putting two small classes together would have made better use of the rooms and teachers while giving more stimulus to the children. The happy outcome was that changes were made, and the teachers felt stronger for having stated their problem, analyzed it, and taken steps toward a constructive solution.

I am constantly amazed that an untrained teacher will attempt to work under conditions which a professional would never tolerate. Sometimes imagination on the teacher's part will work wonders, but it is no substitute for an administration that cares, provides, and gives teachers their due. The prototype for the Sunday School teacher is often the Hebrew slaves in Egypt making bricks without straw. Perhaps governing boards should read and meditate on Exodus 1.

If the attractiveness of a room is important, so is the equipment: comfortable chairs and tables, shelf space to display books attractively, wall space for chalkboard and for bulletin board, cabinet space to keep the room neat and supplies readily available. Teachers should never have to buy their own supplies. They might not begrudge a few dollars, but it would be another indication of the low esteem in which their work is held.

Training Teachers

The third step is personal, individualized training. New teachers begin at varying stages of development. Some have taught previously but in a different setting or with different materials. Others have never taught. Some are apprehensive, others are curious, still others are eager for the new experience. They cannot be treated alike. If children are to be treated as unique individuals, so are teachers. That is why the telephone may be your best tool. People like to talk on the phone; they can express both ideas and feelings in a sort of halfway anonymity. They cannot see or be seen by the person to whom they speak. This frees them. Encourage teachers to phone the superintendent or director of Christian education. Make it possible for a teacher to begin as a helper, preferably on a team that prepares together so that the new teacher can get the feel of the process without having full responsibility.

The next step is team teaching. A co-teacher has responsibility but receives support. Sometimes two new teachers would like to be co-teachers, prefering to share the uncertainty of newness with each other rather than with an experienced teacher. A variant is to have a more experienced teacher be a partner to a new teacher. This is not necessarily someone teaching the same age group. It might be a friend of the new teacher or the person who recruited the new teacher. This would be someone who knows the church, can obtain needed materials, answer questions, and reassure.

This also takes part of the support task from the director or superintendent who could not do this adequately if too many teachers were under his or her care. If you have a large administrative setup, the department superintendents would be the natural persons for the job. I stress this because Sunday School work has often been program oriented rather than person oriented. Superintendents were expected to keep records, hand out supplies, see that classes were covered, deal with discipline problems, and meet parents of new children. The whole stress of this chapter—and the book—is that the work of anyone in the Sunday School is primarily that of helping fellow Christians who happen to be teaching.

Encouragement alone is not enough. The new teacher has a specific job to do and needs to know about methods, materials, and all kinds of resources. Not all teachers need to know the same things. Someone should make a habit of finding clippings, copies of selected magazine articles, or books which would speak to a teacher's specific need. This might be a new method, a list of filmstrips, or background for biblical study. Such a resource person could become invaluable for any Sunday School teacher.

Sometimes a superintendent's visit or that of a director to a class may be helpful to the teacher. I say this with hesitation. I like to visit a class so that I know what problems a teacher faces and can be more realistic when asked for help. Teachers, however, often believe that the superintendent is watching them, not the class, and they become anxious. Then the visit becomes uncomfortable for everyone. It could be a valuable tool for helping, but you have to know the teacher. The teacher must trust you, and a new teacher must have developed some basic security and rapport with the class.

The fourth point is to arrange a teaching situation which is not beyond the new teacher. It may seem unnecessary to say this, but don't throw the new teacher to a difficult class. No matter how desperately a class needs a teacher, the problem is only made worse by not waiting until the right person comes along. Be honest in telling a teacher what a class may be like, although it is not fair to predispose a teacher in advance to think of a group as easy or difficult. It takes all kinds of children to make a class.

Nor does this mean that you should separate boys and girls into separate classes on the theory that girls are easier to deal with. Both are easier to handle when they are together, and that is the way life usually is for them at home and at school, even though there are a few years during which they may prefer to play in segregated groups.

Make help available to the beginning teacher or to any teacher who might be having a difficult time. This could happen because one or two children in a class are difficult, or because a group suddenly grew too large. It could even happen at the end of a rainy week when all the children are in an edgy mood.

Finally, encourage a new teacher to take on further responsibility as a readiness to do so appears. Encourage one to try new methods, to call on parents in person or by telephone, to invite new children, or to use an increasingly flexible classroom schedule. The reward is the satisfaction of a group happily learning together and the praise of others who care enough to speak an encouraging word.

A fifth point is to give teachers opportunities to know each other, share their concerns, have personal enrichment, and develop tools for teaching. Traditional teachers' meetings do that. The monthly occasion (perhaps a supper meeting) is when business is discussed and some form of teacher training used—a resource speaker, film, or workshop for practicing methods. Fit the occasion to the lives of your teachers. If a meeting time becomes difficult, make this a quarterly event. At other times, meet in small groups. The value of a meeting with all teachers is that they become aware of sharing a common task and get to know one another. It also makes practical the use of a film or the presence of an outside speaker. For specific training, the small group may be preferable, gathering a teaching team or those who work with one age-group. Since the members of a group will want to meet to plan a unit, decide what resources are needed and outline how they will share the work. Parents frequently find mornings to be the best meeting time; the preschoolers can accompany them and the other children are at school. For the working parents and other adults, a compromise may be necessary—evenings or Saturday mornings.

There are other forms of training I hope your teachers will want. An all-day meeting with a resource person provides leisure to really dig into questions. The weekend or week-long conference should be available and paid for by the church. This might be a family conference. Getting together with other Sunday School teachers in the community can be a useful form of teacher training because the children frequently attend the same schools, and teachers of elementary school children will find that they have much in common despite their different traditions and curricular materials. In recent years, this has been largely an untapped source for encouraging new teachers. The importance of group training lies in the happy combination of study and fellowship.

Hearing What Teachers Say

Another quite different way of encouraging teachers is to give them a voice in policymaking for the Sunday School.

They know the situation better than anyone else does. They need to feel that their work is important enough so that their experience counts outside that one hour on Sunday. This gives them status. They need to be asked more important questions than when the Sunday School picnic should be held. They are closely involved in the impact of the Sunday School and should not feel that others are setting the guidelines that they must follow.

Similarly the relationship of parents can be helpful or harmful to the development of teachers. It is discouraging to care deeply enough about the Christian nurture of children to give time to teaching and then have parents indifferent to what one is trying to do. Worse, many parents take children out of town without even the courtesy of a phone call to the teacher and an offer to help make up the lost session. The teacher must pick up the pieces of a class which may be large one week and discouragingly small the next. Those children present each week have a sense of continuity and can fill in the absentees by reviewing the work. Whatever you can do to help teachers use discontinuity in a creative way saves them from the frustration which sometimes ends in resigning the job. Perhaps you can encourage parents to phone teachers, make up lessons at home, or urge their children to share vacation experiences with the class.

There is also the parent who doesn't like what is being done in Sunday School. You must protect the teacher from the complaint and at the same time express appreciation that a parent takes an interest in what is going on. You might also find ways of involving such parents in a positive way without interfering with the teacher's work.

Finally, a teacher needs the opportunity for refreshment—adult groups for their own development such as Bible study groups, theological inquiry classes, retreats, or prayer groups. Be sure that teachers have opportunities to attend church serivces. The popular family service which enables parents to attend may prevent teachers from participation in morning worship. On the other hand, holding Sunday School sessions and church services at separate times may leave a parent or teacher no way to care for the family while attending church. Later we will look at the possibility of group experiences for children during part of the church hour (chapter 7).

Be sure that the church prays for teachers, new and experienced; that they are remembered in morning worship; that individuals are encouraged to make them part of their own intercessory prayer; and that parents and teachers pray for each other and for those whom they teach.

You may still lose some teachers as soon as you have trained them: jobs change, families move, a new baby arrives. Your consolation will have to be in the hope that they will be useful elsewhere, and that someone else, already trained, will move into their places.

Summary

Here is a list of ways to keep teachers. How many do you use?

1. Make specific efforts to encourage them and keep morale high.
2. Provide adequate money for rooms and equipment.
3. Give personalized training and find special resources.
4. Put a teacher with a class that that person is likely to be able to handle.
5. Provide opportunities for personal enrichment, study, and fellowship.

6. Give teachers a voice in policymaking.
7. Encourage supportive relationships from parents.
8. Provide opportunities for refreshment in worship and study.

4
Getting and Keeping Pupils

The other half of the teaching team, so to speak, is the pupils. If the teachers have been your problem, it might surprise you to know that some Sunday Schools have faded out of existence for lack of pupils. How do you prevent such a disaster? Or, how do you build up enrollment in a new parish?

You begin with the families you have—list their children and young people, and remember that adults are also learners. You enroll children at birth. Hopefully, you have presented new parents with preparatory material even before the baby's arrival. This is the time to offer help, as parents think ahead to the religious nurture of the new child, along with their concern about other areas of growth. Happy is the church with someone who can make this group into a fellowship, by visiting, sending an occasional letter, remembering birthdays, and even establishing a nursery at church. Include also the offer of babysitting for important meetings that parents might want to attend.

One church has Wednesday-morning-out for mothers. They bring their preschool children for a program while they have coffee together and a meeting with a reading discussion or outside speaker or another form of program to help with the first steps in religious development. Such efforts form a tie until the time when a child is ready for more formal nursery-kindergarten groups.

Welcome New Families

How you enroll new children is an important factor in their feeling at home in the church. Some families moving into a new community come to church almost immediately. I hope you meet them in a comfortable, attractive setting and ask in a concerned but not probing way for the basic information you need: the names of the parents and their work, the names and ages of their children, previous church affiliation, address, and telephone number. Talk about their former church and community; the past is important when one has just moved into a new setting. The new child is not ready yet to relinquish it. Tell something about your Sunday School, stressing probable similarities to the former experience. Be sure that someone takes the child to the classroom and that the teacher gives a warm reception. Some teachers need to be reminded how to greet newcomers.

If the parents have come, you will want to make them feel welcome and keyed into what you are doing. Later be sure that someone calls on the family at home to learn about their former home, the hopes for living in the new community, and the expectations for their church relationship. This will give you further information for the records. This first meeting will be remembered by the newcomers and will be an important factor in their decision to become involved in your parish or to shop further.

At this point you begin to feel conscious of a difference. Some children come from active church families; others are sent to Sunday School by parents who are inactive in the church community. Yet the latter children may be just as eager as the former. Try not to favor the church-family child; avoid sending messages home through mother when you see her at a meeting during the week. Whether or not your concern for a child seems to be appreciated by the parents, you know that God has intentions for each child. You will need to make special efforts toward the child whose parents seem indifferent. Make a point of greeting a parent who brings a child and returns after the session. When a parent never appears, strike up a telephone acquaintance. Contacts between the church and this home are important. Remember that these parents care enough about the child's religious nurture to desire the Sunday School experience even though they feel no personal need for the church.

You will also want to remember that some of the casual references in class could make this child feel like an outsider because of assuming a family-at-church situation: families sitting together in church, family prayer or Bible reading. The child needs to feel that what parents do is good and that the practices of religiously oriented families are not to be regarded as condemning the nonobservant family. You can always hope that this family will someday become participants in the life of the church and observe Christian practices at home.

There is another aspect to recruiting new pupils. Some of you live in growing neighborhoods with new people arriving all the time. Others are in stable neighborhoods where people seldom move. Perhaps the population is older, and there will be no spectacular growth. There are still children outside the Sunday School. It is well to remember that the Sunday School is an important factor in church extension. I once belonged to a church which began almost a century ago as a Sunday School and did not hold church services for several years. Now it is a strong witness in its community, but it began with a concern for the children in a new suburb.

How do you attract new pupils? The obvious beginning is with the children you have. Ask them what Sunday Schools other children in their neighborhood attend. Are there children in their class at school who do not go to Sunday School? Would they like to have an invitation to attend? It might be practical to have a visitors' Sunday. Newcomers might feel more comfortable when there were several of them in a class.

Seeking Pupils

You could encourage adult members to think about their neighborhood. Can they call to mind families without a church home? Is there some parish event to which such families could be invited in order to become acquainted with you? Would these members invite such families to attend church? If parents are reluctant to come, frequently they are happy to have their children be your guests at Sunday School and at the church service. If some of your members are hesitant to contact unchurched people in their neighborhood, someone else might be given the name and address to extend the invitation. It is helpful to have a visiting committee of warm, outgoing people who can feel at ease inviting others. One of the more important points in attracting newcomers is to select as their first visitors people with gifts of friendliness.

Another important way of attracting new pupils is through special programs. Vacation Bible School immediately comes to mind because it has become a community fixture. Children love to have something to do in summer, and parents are happy for this form of activity. If you advertise widely, you will attract others. Promotion requires special abilities. You need people for this task. Use posters, your local newspaper, and local radio and television stations. Some regard such announcements as a public service. Weekday programs or a Saturday morning program, especially if these differ in format and materials from regular Sunday School sessions, will also attract nonchurch children.

There are some parents who want religion for their children but who want it to seem unconnected with church. Sunday and Sunday School mean church to them. A similar program in the same building on a weekday afternoon or Saturday seems less official. Some churches have a late afternoon and early evening program for older children, combining choir, study, games, and supper. There are many possible variations. Only you can find the best plan because it depends on school and afterschool programs, children's involvement in out-of-school activities, such as music lessons, and the weekend habits of families.

Summer camping programs or weekend camping for older boys and girls is another unusual program likely to attract the friends of your regular children. These require people with special abilities, imagination to develop a program, and money to make it succeed. This is part of your mission of community outreach.

Encouraging Attendance

So far we have been mainly talking about enrollment. That is not the whole story! Regular attendance is vital and some Sunday Schools have a dismal record. Do we have to accept a seasonal curve in which attendance peaks at Christmas, drops during January, picks up during Lent, and trails off after Easter? What can you do during low periods? Why have parents so casual an attitude toward attendance? A family who moved last summer from the Midwest to a New England community felt quite lost upon arrival to find that Sunday Schools were closed until September. This may be a regional custom and not observed by all churches, but it raises questions as to the seriousness with which Christian commitment is taken when a church bulletin board welcomes visitors with the notice Closed for This Month.

Let it be said again that the basic factor is what happens during a class session. There are children who insist on getting to Sunday School every week. Parents have noted with amazement that a child objected strongly to going away weekends because there was so much going on at church. This puts us in a quandary. We want them to come, but we could hardly say that the child's wishes should form the sole basis for a family's decision. Here is where the relationship of understanding between home and church is important.

Why would a child be so eager to be present at Sunday School? To begin with, there is a teacher whose love is felt and through whom God's love is known. Then there is a lively class session which has a focus and through which the child feels a sense of accomplishment. There is a room rich with materials, necessary equipment, and the possibility of imaginative methods through which the child's curiosity and interest are challenged. Children want to know God. Some teachers and some classes help.

There must also be a climate of mutual friendship and helpfulness in the classroom so that any child feels accepted by the other children: encouraged when afraid, forgiven when bad, praised for good work. The writer remembers a seventh grade class in which each Sunday session opened with class members sharing important events of the week. Absentees were inquired about and cards prepared for them. Some class members usually knew why there was an absence. At the close of the session, class members quietly prayed for one another and their work during the coming week. Each felt that this hour was important for the whole week. The successful class has a sense of purpose; it is meeting the needs and questions of the pupils and dealing with problems.

Begin with the youngest children. If there is a strong class followed by a weak one, the continuity is lost. A child gets out of the habit of attending and recovery the following year may be slow. (This goes back to teacher recruitment and training. How intertwined these questions are!)

Helping Absentees

There is still the problem of what to do about absences. The sick child will welcome having the teacher suggest what went on in the session so that the work can be done at home and nothing is missed. This gives an activity for parent and child and gives parents practice in taking part in religious education. It might even begin to arouse their curiosity and involvement. A phone call or postal card (children love to receive mail) might help.

> Dear John,
>
> You were missed today. We read the story on page 3 in the story book and answered the questions. Perhaps mother or dad could read it to you, and you could talk about it together. I hope you can come next week.
>
> Sincerely,

If the book is not at home, you will need to take or send a copy for use until the child returns to Sunday School.

Summer vacation (or perhaps winter) presents different problems. Encourage families to go to church as they travel or visit, and suggest that these experiences be shared upon their return. Post a map with a piece of yarn stretching from your church to the points representing families' travels. At the side of the map, place church bulletins or the names of churches attended. Summer experiences can be incorporated into early September sessions.

Weekending is something else again and a great trial to teachers. Attendance becomes sporadic, and it is difficult to know how to prepare a session. Morale is low because a class suddenly becomes small. That is the teacher's side of the problem. To some families, weekends are important forms of recreation and relaxation and may be the only time the family is together. This can be a good family experience, and we should not lose sight of that possibility in a concern for Sunday School attendance. Close family interest and cooperation may make possible the use of an option suggested for other vacation times; the family may establish a church base wherever they go for weekends. Many families have a second home in another community. Interact with that church so that the family knows you care and that belonging to the church is not confined to attendance at one location.

Do not assume that weekending is inevitable. Persist in efforts to show parents the importance of the church in their lives and their children's. Help them to realize that children value whatever their parents value, whether it be school, out-of-school activities, or Sunday School. What the family neglects will seem unimportant.

If you are in a community where the pulling power of

weekend activities seems beyond resistance, consider other days for "Sunday" School. With all the associations which the name holds, it does indeed seem tied to the day. Sunday has been accepted and respected for generations as the day for religious activities. This is no longer so. If you have decided by careful, responsible searching that many children are being neglected through the limitation of the Sunday School, consider an auxiliary weekday session, not to replace the Sunday session which is still important to many, but to serve the needs of those now left out by changing family habits.

Some churches have successfully begun a family program on a midweek evening. (Wednesday night has long been an established time for church services.) The program begins with supper to which all bring food, followed by worship, a family-oriented program (film, story, or speaker), and sometimes small groups, either age-graded or intergenerational, to discuss the earlier presentation or explore meanings through creative activities. Parents and children learn together, and parents learn how to talk about their faith with their children.

Parents Teach Religion

This brings up the question of the family's responsibility for Christian nurture. Many parents have begun this long before the child reaches school age by teaching an evening prayer, saying grace before meals, and listening to the big questions which small children ask. Here is where a wise person or couple is needed to head the nursery. As children grow older, it is understandable that parents feel some formal teaching can be done more effectively by the Sunday

School. There is real value in hearing the gospel story from several persons. Teachers are witnesses in ways which differ from parents. Children also learn from one another in the class session.

The distinctive role of parents lies in the way faith is learned through family life: shared celebrations such as thanksgiving before meals, Christmas eve and Christmas rituals, the celebration of Easter, the observance of birthdays and other anniversaries, the special quality of the opening and closing days of school. Some families gather each day for Scripture reading and prayer. The home is the place where questions come spontaneously; such as the why questions little children ask about life, love, death, and God. These can be answered in a simple witness to faith. Wrongdoing, forgiveness, and restoration are vital, everyday, family experiences through which the redemptive love of God is shown.

Loving relationships between parents and concerned care between parents and children are constant reminders and witnesses to God who shows himself in these ways. "We love because he first loved us," and in showing love, we are giving to others what God is always giving to every person. Parents can enrich such learning by reading Bible stories, using some of the lovely collections of prayer and praise, and teaching hymns.

Parents who worship in the congregation each Sunday are showing that this is of vital importance in their lives. They are the ones best fitted to introduce their children, bringing the youngest occasionally for part of the service and always for special services. This shared experience will help them in answering children's questions and explaining parts of the service. In this way, the child finds a place among the company of the faithful.

The role of parents in the Sunday School varies. Some may become teachers or helping teachers. Others have special skills that they should be invited to share. Children are happy to see their parents included in special ways, and parents have an opportunity to see how the Sunday School works. Some use their skills during the week. Once, when I was visiting a family, the mother invited the class to have a cookout in the yard so that I, their teacher, and the children could get acquainted informally at the beginning of the year. It was a wonderful idea and the more appreciated because she offered it. The same thing happened the next year with another class. Perhaps you will always find such a family in each class!

Friendly relationships between parents and teachers are a great help in maintaining enrollment and attendance. When parents know a teacher and are sensitive to the hard work he or she has put into the class on behalf of their children, many will be conscientious in wanting to assist. They will realize that regular attendance is important and that continuity, whether through attendance wherever they are travelling or through the use of homework, is much appreciated.

Summary

So, enrollment is important. Let's review the steps:

1. Make a good first impression on new parents by who greets them and where and how you show interest in their former home and their coming to your community and church.
2. Keep in close touch with parents who do not attend church, remembering that concern motivates them to send the children.

3. Reach into the community for new children by finding out who in the neighborhoods where your people live are unattached to any church.
4. Have special events that will atttract newcomers —such as weekday or vacation programs and introductory family events at church.

How to keep up attendance:

1. Have the kind of teachers and class that will keep children coming.
2. Encourage parents to aid continuity by attending church when away and teaching the lesson to the child when absent.
3. Make friends with parents and use their skills in the Sunday School program.
4. Have an auxiliary weekday program for children or for families.

Rewards

Children like to be with other children, are curious to learn, and enjoy coming to a Sunday School program which is interesting. Some churches supplement these satisfactions with a tangible reward program of some kind. After all, everyone likes payment, gifts, or honors for work accomplished. If you have used such a system with success, remember three things:

1. There is no substitute for a good teaching program. It is hollow to keep children coming for perfect attendance when they are not learning anything or if they are learning the wrong thing, such as how to outwit the teacher. Few adults are happy in a job

simply because of the money; the job must have its own satisfaction. So with children's work.

2. Be concerned about children for whom the reward itself becomes the object. One young man had fifteen bars attached to his attendance pin. His father was the church sexton and lived in the building. Doubtless he enjoyed Sunday School, but it was certainly easy to get there. Children *should* be absent when sick and not bring infections to others.
3. The pressure for attendance should not be so great as to cause conflict in a family. There are good reasons why children must be absent, and the reward program should acknowledge this fact.

Now ask yourself how a system of rewards can be used constructively to encourage learning, growth, and religious development.

5
The Concerned Committee

You probably realize by now that this book has been all about people. Sometimes we think of Sunday School as an organization or a program. Of course it *is* an organization and it *has* a program, but the point of organization is to smooth the process. The program, hopefully, is designed for people. That is why we are first talking about people: teachers, pupils, and parents.

In this chapter, we want to emphasize the fact that these people who make up the Sunday School are a lonely group, however large. They are on an island—so to speak—unless there are lots of backup people willing to work toward the fulfillment of the goals. A congregation may begin as a Sunday School, but a Sunday School cannot continue for long unless it is part of a whole church. Many people need to care about its welfare.

Begin by looking at the fact that things get accomplished in any group because there are people with power, people with authority. Sometimes money talks, as the saying goes. Sometimes a strong personality draws people (*charisma* is the popular word). Sometimes it is the ability to get things done either through individual initiative and skill in problem solving or because someone is in a position to open doors. Every church has an inner core of people responsible for its welfare. The members are highly esteemed and have a sense of importance. There is status in being elected to this board, and it has real power. It draws up a budget and frequently the amount of money given for an enterprise determines the extent of the program's effectiveness and says clearly what activities are considered important in the life of that church.

Speaking of Power

Where does religious education, specifically the Sunday School, come in the thinking of your governing board? How much money is allocated? How does this fit proportionately to other sums allocated in the budget? Is there anyone on this board who has a close relationship to the Sunday School as parent, teacher, or member of the religious education board? Is the minister interested in the Sunday School? These are important questions and if the answer to any of them is *no*, you are in trouble—but at least there is room for improvement.

Some ministers are interested but never see the Sunday School in action because it meets at the same time as the church service. Some pastors have two churches, and this presents the same problem. Others have had unhappy experiences in their youth, trying to teach a class with which they were unable to cope. If the seminary student was paid for teaching, the most difficult class was chosen, and this inexperienced young person found the year so unpleasant that the resolve was made thenceforth to delegate the Sunday School to anyone else available. Churches employing seminary students should realize that they, as parishes, are helping to form future ministers. This is a privilege, and these students need all the wise guidance you can give them.

The minister is at the head of the authority structure. He or she is a member of the governing board and in many denominations chairperson at its meetings. This is the person who can speak in behalf of the Sunday School when the budget is being made, who knows which people should be asked to teach, and who can suggest concerned persons as members for the governing board. This is the person most knowledgeable about Scripture and theology to be a resource person for teachers, parents, and other adult groups. If such skills were asked for more frequently, your minister would spend more time in reading and study and this would be an enriching experience for all.

Let's look at the governing board itself. In addition to setting up the budget, where each interest has to press its cause, there are other responsibilities. One is the care and use of the building and its furnishings. Do rooms need painting in order to be attractive? Do you wish the children could come into the lovely church living room for story time or that this room could be used for a junior high discussion group? Do you need outdoor equipment for a summer program? Are tables worn and chairs uncomfortable? Is there a conflict with a group which uses the rooms during the week? Here is the committee on which you need an advocate.

This group also sets programs. It can help to make special events important such as a film-discussion series, a family supper, or a workshop. If you frequently bring your needs before this committee, your plans will become important in their thinking, and this will eventually become reflected in the budget. You should have a member of this board on the religious education committee, someone who will report from your committee to the governing board and bring to you any counsels from the board.

The women of the church form another group who can be of help to you if they share your concern. Women are so often involved in work with people, especially with children and young people, that they will gladly become your allies. They are frequently guardians of one beautifully appointed room and will be happy to let you use it if you will guarantee that the users will respect the furnishings. They keep the kitchen in order and quite properly want other people to keep the room clean and the equipment in working order. They will be glad to let you use it for preparing coffee or for a properly supervised young people's supper. This is part of their stewardship, and if you understand this, the women can be very helpful to you and your program in the use of the rooms under their care.

Also, the women raise and administer a large budget. While the governing board should bear the primary financial responsibility for the Sunday School, the women's group is usually happy to help with special projects such as equipment for the small children, a particular collection of books, a new supply or file cabinet, curtains to make rooms attractive, a rug for the children's room, and conference scholarships for children, young people, or teachers. Keep the officers of the women's groups informed of your goals, plans, and programs. Many women's groups have one elected officer who is a liaison with the Sunday School. Occasionally, a Sunday School is so weak that even mothers on the women's board fail to be conscious of its needs. I know several mothers who permitted the nursery room to be half-closed off with rummage sale materials until it was pointed out to them that they had rights as mothers and Sunday School teachers in behalf of the children. Then it was found that materials could be kept elsewhere. It may shock you to realize that sometimes people you would expect to pursue the needs of the Sunday School do not do so. They too have accepted its inferior status.

The Religious Education Committee

The key group of concerned people are those on the religious education committee or commission, as some call it. This is an elected committee with regularly scheduled meetings whose members serve on a term basis. It should include men and women of all ages. Although a community school board is composed of people outside the daily life of the school, I have come to feel that this is not the best example to follow. Rather, the board should include teachers, parents, young people, official board members, and people from the congregation with deep spiritual gifts and backgrounds in education or administration. The minister, director of Christian education, and Sunday School superintendent are also members.

Their basic task is to support and strengthen the work of the Sunday School. They assure teachers that the whole church backs their work. In so far as members are active in other church groups, they can help solve some of the problems which interfere with the successful operation of the Sunday School. They have skills; they know people. It is wonderful how a concerned board member can lift a load from the shoulders of the superintendent. They raise morale by their faithful attendance and the serious consideration they give to regularly called meetings. This says clearly to everyone involved in the Sunday School that somebody cares and works for them beyond the Sunday morning session.

The main function of this group is policymaking. The final statement of goals is their work. Basic decisions about curriculum are their responsibility in consultation with teachers and clergy: the type of material, whether to use a complete series or to choose courses from more than one source, which series to use, and setting guidelines when teachers are given initiative. If you have a professional director of Christian education, this person will be competent to make decisions and recommendations.

The religious education committee also sets programs and evaluates the accomplishments at the close of a year, surveying weaknesses and strengths and deciding the emphases for the next year. Is better work needed with young people? Should there be more emphasis on families? Are more diverse learning opportunities indicated for adults? If teacher turnover is large, this is the group to discover the reasons and suggest remedies (see chapter 2). If there are attendance problems, this committee seeks causes and solutions. It recommends teacher training opportunities, promotes camps and conferences, and decides on the nature of summer or weekday teaching programs.

Special Tasks

Outreach is another responsibility. Is the Sunday School missing opportunities or neglecting obligations toward children in the neighborhood? Should you be working with other churches in joint programs for special occasions or teacher training?

The religious education committee should be concerned about informing the whole congregation of what is going on in the Sunday School. The chairperson has the responsibility for preparing a vigorous report at the annual meeting. The work can also be presented at a special event such as a church supper, visiting day at Sunday School, or an evening program for parents, teachers, and other members.

Keeping morale high is another responsibility; it is important for superintendents and teachers to know that board members care and are giving every kind of support, especially in talking up the Sunday School among the whole congregation. One way is to initiate special events for teachers, such as some act of recognition at the close of the year.

Communication is another aspect of caring. Report newsworthy decisions through whatever form of parish paper, letter, or bulletin you have. Be sure that the results of their meeting are first shared with the Sunday School people before being made public information. Committee members might offer to be resource persons for teachers, to help in class, or to share their skills in teacher training. Consider inviting one or more members of the board to regular teacher meetings to deepen their understanding of the task. If they are to be boosters, they have to have firsthand information.

One of the serious jobs of this board is to plan a budget in consultation with the superintendent and/or department heads who would know teacher needs. Sometimes teachers and superintendents are hesitant to make requests and feel that they should make do with what is available. An effective board is generous, encouraging Sunday School leaders to think big and to expand in whatever way will improve their work. A tightfisted board lacks faith and has a feeble sense of mission as well as a low image of the Sunday School it is supposed to serve. If you have that kind of a board, it is time to plan strategy for getting new people in the next election!

People Who Help

When you are a large enough school to need the expertise of a trained religious education director (or coordinator or consultant), a board with vision will be willing to consider this possibility. Their task is to screen candidates and make the choice. It then becomes their responsibility to introduce this person to the life and work of the church, smooth the way while the job is developing, and stand 100 percent in back of the director. This gives your professional person the encouragement necessary to achieve a position in the parish from which to carry out plans with a sense of authority to match the responsibility. The board works in tandem with minister and director, mediating between them in order that there may be a good working relationship, each understanding the intentions of the other.

The board is also responsible for appointing and supporting the Sunday School superintendent. The board will have its own secretary to keep records of actions taken at the meeting and to carry on correspondence. Its treasurer will keep the accounts in order to know in any month how much of the budget has been spent and how much remains. Although the budget is planned by the board, it is responsible to the whole church in its budgeting and to the Sunday School people who need to know where they stand as they make decisions as to when to buy a particular item.

On major expenditures, only the board can make a final decision. Some spending decisions are basically policy decisions: to develop a resource center as an extension of the library, to make a little-used room into a youth center, to recommend to the governing board that a day nursery be permitted to operate in the building, or that the church establish a weekday kindergarten.

Finally, a board should study their task and grow in the ability to function effectively. A book like this would help them understand the breadth of Sunday School activities, whether they discussed it together or simply agreed individually to read it. A policy paper from your denominational board could help to enlarge their vision. Some knowledge of the basis for the curriculum you use would help board members understand and sympathize with the task teachers have. Some board members would welcome an invitation to special training opportunities made available to teachers. A conference leader would be helped by the information brought by board members.

Someday you may need to make a survey to discover potential members, uncover teaching talent, find available resource persons, or sample parent opinion on the work or goals of the Sunday School. The board of religious education is the group to initiate, conduct, and collate results and make deductions from such a survey (or make arrangements for this to be done professionally). With such information, they would be prepared to make recommendations and publicize both the survey and its results. If you hope for a practical response (beyond receiving and filing such a report), the board must feel the sense of responsibility which will make such a survey a positive contribution toward improving the work of the Sunday School.

Others Also Help

So far we have talked about concerned groups: the governing board, the religious education committee, the women's group, and the clergy. Many of you will have a valuable, potential resource in whoever plays the organ and/or directs music. This person might develop in children a knowledge of good music and can help teachers choose hymns and recordings. Some organists with an ability to relate to children and time to spare for the church school may offer to teach hymns in the children's classes. This would be a great help for the ungraded class we talked about earlier. What fun to take one whole session for a hymn-sing for all the children! (More about that later.)

Finally, you will need the loving support of the whole church. Everyone must feel that what is happening in the Sunday School is very important. In my experience, the strongest work in religious education is done by groups who have a sense of the vital importance of the task, who feel that the nurture of children is a task laid upon them by God. Roman Catholics have this. Parochial schools may decline, CCD classes may seem inadequate, but no one concludes that formal teaching should be abandoned and new ways be tried in the hope of discovering a successful formula. The Sunday School, Saturday School, or other weekday school with volunteer teachers may not turn out to be all that is hoped for, but commitment to the task continues strong. Evangelicals also have this firm sense of commitment to a God-given task. Each child is to be nurtured toward personal commitment to Christ as Lord. This is the basis for every teacher's loving witness and persistent faithfulness in teaching. Only on this kind of foundation can any educational program be successful.

Summary

A list of concerned groups and individuals:

1. Within the congregation, there are the governing board, the minister, and the women's group.
2. The religious education committee.
3. Others who help include the organist/choir director, parents, and members of the congregation.

6
Running the Sunday School

This is basically a description of the persons who are needed in order that the program may run smoothly. Organization is important. Taking care of details is important. In the best organization, no one is really conscious that any organizing is taking place. This means that you need a special person in charge: one who likes people, is relaxed, does not get anxious, and does not communicate fears to others, who persuades rather than commands. When the Sunday School is running smoothly, each job seems easier and people feel more secure.

The Superintendent

For example, when a new child comes into a poorly organized school, the family can wander around for a long time, feeling more forlorn with each passing minute, simply looking for a place to stay. What an introduction! The well-organized Sunday School has a superintendent who is looking for the stranger, ready to extend a welcoming hand to parents, an arm to comfort the child, and guidance to the church school secretary (a friendly person who is located in a pleasant place where the family can sit down to give the needed information). They will be personally guided and introduced into the child's classroom. The newcomer is not conscious of the process which produced this pleasant result, but it included several special people: the superintendent with a warm welcome, the secretary who asks questions with genuine interest and not as if it were an interrogation, the guide who takes the family to classes, and the teachers who receive them. In back of this are the people responsible for finding friendly Sunday School people and helping them to understand their role.

Even when a professional is in charge of religious education, you will need as superintendent (by whatever title known) a knowledgeable person whose skills are in facilitating the administration, encouraging and supporting the people involved, and being aware of the situation to be sure everything goes smoothly.

The director of Christian education (consultant, coordinator) is an important resource person who can go into a classroom upon invitation, meet with new parents, work with a new teacher, or facilitate the beginning of a new program. The professional needs to be freed from details in order that these specialized skills may be used to fullest advantage. The superintendent is a different kind of skilled person, smoothing relationships and situations. The superintendent (and director if you have both) greets teachers on arrival and seeks them as they leave (see chapter 2). Support and encouragement for teachers is an important and, hopefully, a joyous part of the job. The superintendent makes sure that secretary and treasurer understand their tasks. This person needs organizing skills to match rooms to classes in accordance with the needs of a group. (For example, there should be no assigned room for second grade unless all rooms are the same size.) The superintendent will be the one to ask the women's group for help, clue the religious education committee into needs, and relate the Sunday School to the governing board.

Another relationship the superintendent has is with parents. Some come to complain of a teacher and need tactful understanding which will acknowledge their distress while protecting the teacher's intentions. Parents want to know that someone has overall supervision of the Sunday School; so it is helpful to have a superintendent with a knack for remembering names and faces who can get acquainted with the parents who come on Sunday morning. The superintendent is the person who protects teachers from interruption during the session: from the secretary who wants to push an attendance book through the door, the usher who wants to make an announcement, or the parent who has come five minutes early for a child. You can see that the superintendent really needs to be everywhere at once! One is surely in the midst of things, and some people love that kind of job.

The Secretary—Treasurer

The superintendent is a key person, but the effective one does not try to do everything. The secretary is an important helper: pleasant, eager to be useful, and willing to do detailed work, but with enough self-assurance not to let people push all the work in that direction. The secretary may not be the person who designs the record-keeping procedures but is the one to administer them.

You will want a permanent record card so that you know about a child's family and church background. You will want a class attendance book. On Sunday morning, these should be either in a teacher's box in the office or at a convenient place in the classroom before the session begins. The teacher can leave it in the office at the close of the session. No matter how impatient someone may be to compile attendance figures, the session should not be interrupted for this purpose. Teachers may, if they wish, agree that early in the session a helping teacher or one of the pupils will return the book to the office.

The same advice goes for the collection of offering envelopes. If the children have been in the church service, they participate in the offertory there. If you have a Sunday School worship service or a departmental one, the offering has been received then. Those who have simply a class session will need to treat the mechanics of the offering as they do the attendance—to be returned to the office at an agreed-upon time. The teacher will then have to decide how to incorporate receiving the offering into the session. For some it becomes part of the worship service. Others ask pupils to deposit it upon arrival in the offering plate or large envelope.

The secretary also takes care of correspondence, sending out notices of meetings, ordering materials, and also preparing publicity releases at the request of the superintendent. This might mean sending information for the church paper or information about Sunday School events to a local newspaper, announcements for the minister to make, or notes for the children to take home.

Another essential person is the treasurer. Although the

money is allocated in the church budget, the Sunday School is steward of these funds and must make an annual accounting. Keeping the books requires a person with technical knowledge. The Sunday School treasurer, however, is more than an accountant, for this is not a business but a living and sensitive part of the church. The practical helpfulness of the treasurer to the people in the Sunday School is to keep them alerted to how much money they have available in each category. Should all the money allocated to equipment be spent to replace furniture in the primary room? Is there enough money both for buying course books for each child and for buying extra reading books?

Such questions require decisions by the teachers. As the year ends, the treasurer can alert the Sunday School to categories in which spending needs to be slowed down—if not ended. Note the word *alert*. The treasurer is not a manager whose words and manner give the impression of controlling what goes on through the account books. The good treasurer helps people develop wise spending patterns without telling them when and how to spend the money.

Resource Persons

Other resource persons are needed. If your Sunday School is small, you may want to combine functions. Sometimes people with special skills are looking for a way to serve. The first person who comes to mind is a roving helper. In the course of any Sunday, there will be at least one child not getting along in the classroom. This distracts the other children and may leave a teacher completely at wit's end. The teacher may try the pressure of authority and only make things worse. The child feels rejected; the teacher defeated. Sending the child to the superintendent as ultimate authority and punisher is no solution. The child has a problem and needs help. Here is where a firm and loving person can assure the child that this is not the best place to be since nobody is getting along well and suggest that they do something together. If you have a library or resource room, this is the perfect place to find something to do: pictures to look at, a book to read together, or a Bible puzzle to put together. In one Sunday School, the person in charge of the library took this responsibility as troubleshooter. It was a natural combination. The library was quiet, and anyone in there was on business. It is a good place to talk if that is what the child needs.

Another resource person is the permanent substitute: one person who will appear on Sunday morning just in case someone has to be absent. If you have team teaching, substituting does not require special preparation but only the ability to fit into a situation as needed. If you have a pool of teachers in training or teachers temporarily retired from teaching, several substitutes may be on telephone alert. Some Sunday Schools promise teachers a two or three year term of teaching followed by a year off.

There could be a person in charge of resources, whether these be on a shelf or in a whole room. Today, as you know, libraries include more than books. There may be a picture and poster collection, slides and filmstrips, cassettes and catalogs listing available resources from the denomination, council of churches, or state library. There may also be recordings and tapes. Someone needs to have the care of this equipment: to store it, run it, be sure that it is in good order, and to teach others how to use it. Sometimes the most knowledgeable person in this area is a teenager; so you may want to divide the resource activities among a committee.

The selection of resources is as important as their care.

Teachers should be the primary selectors, eager to enrich their teaching. The church librarian has available lists to help in the selection; denominational or national church library associations publish such lists. Some member of this resource committee should be skilled in promotion: able to display books attractively, make posters and charts which suggest the use of various resources, and be helpful in steering teachers and pupils to useful materials. Every teachers' meeting should be an opportunity for the resource person to share new and helpful ideas.

You will say that this is a setup for a large church. Not so. It is simply a description of the work needed for an effective Sunday School. You must develop the ingenuity to picture people in your church in these roles or in combinations of roles. If you use many people, then each is required to give less time. This encourages some to accept a task. You, however, may have a few people with skill and plenty of time. Then all kinds of combinations are possible, such as a secretary-treasurer. One resource person can combine the skills of troubleshooter and substitute teacher. Only the roles are described. The persons to fill them will vary with the situation.

The Building

One other essential factor is the setting. You know that a Sunday School makes an immediate impression when you first enter. In fact, you can go into the empty rooms on Monday morning and have a pretty clear picture of what did or did not go on during Sunday morning. What feeling do you want to convey to those who enter the rooms? Will they be functional like a factory or office? Do they display what is being "sold" as in a store? Are there ordered settings as for a conference? Or filled with resources as for a workshop? Is there the informal quality of a home?

Some people are saying that the traditional school room is not necessarily the best way to set up a Sunday School. Religious learning goes beyond intellectual learning and perhaps requires a setting of warmth: the inviting quality of readily available materials and the informality through casual arrangements of tables and chairs. You know that when people sit in rows they respond differently from when they are seated in a semicircle; that when they sit in an open circle of chairs they respond differently from when they sit around a table.

With these ideas in mind, think about how you want your children to receive the Christian faith, remembering that it is caught, not taught. What kind of setting would be most helpful? Do you need bright curtains or simply shuttered windows? Can you afford carpeted flooring which makes possible so many kinds of activities? What space divisions will be most helpful? Do you need to shut out sounds? Then you will need permanent partitions. Do you need simply to shut out sight? Screens and moving bulletin boards will do this. What is the most versatile table you can buy? Folding tables today are sturdy and can be adjusted to any height, serving the preschoolers on Sunday and adults on weekday evenings.

How can a room become multipurpose? (Remember that children's toys can be arranged to make an attractive shelf display when a room is put to other uses.) What could be lovelier for a small child than to sit on the plush rug or curl up on a sofa beside the teacher in a comfortably furnished room? There are times when the kitchen would be the most practical place for an activity period, with broad washable surfaces and plenty of water for easy clean up.

These suggestions are made to help you develop versatility and to become inventive; so that you will put your whole building to its fullest use. Even as I write, I can see in my mind's eye both the suburban church with its multi-roomed parish house and the country church with one basement room capable of providing everything suggested in the previous paragraph. Admittedly, there are some situations in which there is no substitute for money. Neither is there ever a substitute for imagination. Seek out persons in your fellowship who have this gift and who can help to make a welcoming, inviting atmosphere which radiates the joy of Christian faith.

Tools for Learning

The resources offered to teachers and learners are important tools. It is essential to live the Christian life, but people learn through many forms. You begin with curriculum materials. Will you use only one course of study? Maybe, as in the schools, you would rather have several kinds of material available for use than to have all the books from one source. It will give more variety in story, activity, and other methods, and make available several learning levels for each class. This is especially useful if you are using a group-graded or ungraded approach.

If there are thirty children and three teachers, consider getting a teacher manual from each of three publishers which can circulate among the teachers and be used in their joint planning session. Get ten pupil books from each of the three publishers and use these in small groups, for informal table work, and for rotating as take-home readers.

If it is your custom to send something home every week, be sure the material is used. If it is not, you are wasting money.

Unfortunately, the mere presence of a lesson book in a house is not a silent witness any more than it is a source of learning. If take-home material goes only to those who are present on Sunday morning, you are getting even less value for your money. The people who really need it are the ones who are home sick or out of town and did not get what was being taught in class. The shelf of reading books may be your richest source of auxiliary material if you encourage each child to take home a book every week, returning it the next week to exchange it for another book. You could use a few minutes at the beginning of the session to share reading so that pupils will be encouraged to increase their use of books.

You will also want supplies in large packages because this is the least expensive way to buy: manila paper, colored construction paper, powder or poster paints, large and small crayons, newsprint, and found materials, useful for all sorts of creative activities. Some Sunday Schools spend a lot of money on activities which require only minimal thought and skill on the part of the children: cut and paste or crayoning. These have their occasional use, but the teaching value is not equal to the cost. When a child thinks about a story and tells it in words and drawings, the meaning *to the child* is being expressed. The child is being given opportunity to communicate the story to others. The teacher can see how much has been understood.

Realize then, that the preconstructed activity which requires little work in order to produce a finished product gives some satisfaction but is particularly useful as a weekday or presession activity. It is no substitute for encouraging the child to reflect and express learning in personal terms.

Summary

Now for an outline of the essential people for an effective Sunday School.

1. Superintendent: supports and encourages teachers, sees that procedures are well-organized and run smoothly, mediates between parents, teachers, and children with problems.
2. Secretary: keeps enrollment and attendance records, carries on correspondence, makes supplies easily accessible to teachers.
3. Treasurer: keeps financial records, disburses funds as required, keeps superintendent and teachers aware of what money is available for various purposes.
4. Resource persons: a roving helper to work with children who are disturbing a class; a substitute teacher to fill in on short notice; a resource person to form, make available, and encourage the use of varied materials with teachers, pupils, and parents; an audio-visual resource person to keep equipment in order, oversee its use, and assist teachers in learning how to use such materials fully.
5. Professional, trained director, coordinator, or consultant: has graduate training in Scripture, theology, education, and religious education for the enrichment of those who are lay leaders in the church's educational work.

The setting should include:

1. Attractive rooms, arranged to make the best use of space for the kind of teaching you need and the

number of children and teachers in the Sunday School.
2. Equipment and furnishings to facilitate teaching.
3. Supplies that encourage creativity.

7
Variety—The Spice of Life

Because the tradition of Sunday as a day set aside for religious purposes is still of some importance, it is good for us to take advantage of it. Many find, however, that even church families set other priorities and that there are good reasons to consider other options.

Sunday Options

We do not always realize how many variations are possible on the use of Sunday. Some churches hold the Sunday School before the morning service; others hold it afterward. A number have one session of one and a half to two hours in which there is interaction between the Sunday School and the church service. In this arrangement, the whole family comes to church at the same time. Usually preschool children go directly to classes while younger primary children stay for part of the service every week, once a month, or occasionally. In this way, they absorb what it means to be part of the worshipping community. Usually they are accompanied by parents, but some sit with teachers.

Children should be helped to understand the service, week by week, either by parents at home or by teachers in the class. Hymns can be learned; a responsive reading can be practised; questions can help them to understand the Scripture lessons. Where there is the tradition of a frequent Communion service, many feel that it is important for children to be present at this central act of worship. Opinions vary as to whether children should stay for the whole service or part; whether they should stay every week or attend only occasionally. Parental wishes should be encouraged. Admittedly, some children sit more quietly than do others. For small children, there is the practical problem of dangling legs, a most uncomfortable position. Happy the child whose church has kneeling benches which can be used for footrests!

At some point during the service, children go to their classes. Adult classes convene at the close of the session. The value of this arrangement is that the entire family can come because there is no reason to stay home because of children. The serious disadvantage is that teachers are deprived of the opportunity to attend the full service of worship unless there is an earlier service or an evening service. Teachers need this spiritual refreshment if they are to continue, week after week, to share their faith with others. The arrangement may have the further defect of leaving only a brief time for classes. It is assumed that there would be no departmental worship service, although prayer together in class can still be an important element. The time can be lengthened if the church service is followed by coffee hour and/or adult study classes.

One variant may make possible all that has been asked for; when the children leave the church service, they go into an ungraded program requiring few teachers. The program could vary from week to week but share a given theme which changed monthly; a film or filmstrip, recordings, hymns or other music for use in the service, informal dramatization of biblical stories, a visit from a resource person to share some special experience, or a special project could supplement the study. Such a general program is feasible only if a full hour for more specific study will be made available at another time, as in the traditional pattern of a Sunday School session held either before or after morning worship.

Let's look at the possibilities for a community where family weekend recreational activities have so undermined the Sunday School that efforts at building parent or pupil loyalty have had no effect.

Some families return late Sunday afternoon and a family evening program could be a possibility. Begin with a simple supper, gather everyone for a service of evening worship, conclude with a family-oriented program in which all can participate, such as story telling or a film presentation. Alternatively, divide into groups, along age-group or intergenerational lines. Sunday evening is also an excellent time for serious adult study groups, whether in homes or at church (see chapter 9).

Weekday Possibilities

Do not overlook the possibility of weekday morning programs. Church buildings—whether one room or twenty—are woefully underused. Expensive to build and maintain, sitting on tax-exempt land, they often represent a serious lack of stewardship. Who needs a special room for one hour a week? On weekday mornings, preschool children and some mothers are free. Consider the mothers'-morning-out program. If you are a large congregation, you could run this in several sections on many mornings. Mothers and children gather for a two-hour session. Children have the kind of activities in which they can learn with other children. Mothers gather separately for coffee and a discussion program with a resource leader. They determine the agenda, and there are numerous possibilities: understanding parenthood, religious development of children, strengthening Christian faith, Bible study, a prayer group, community-oriented study.

Another possible weekday program is the morning nursery school or kindergarten, frequently sponsored by churches when such opportunities are not provided by the public schools. Many have found newcomers attracted to a church which has enough concern for young families to establish such a school. Whole books have been written on the subject; so it is enough to note here that as a matter of policy such a school is responsible to the religious education committee, and its head is appointed by that group. This is Christian education, not simply because it meets in a church building, but because the children are learning good relationships and receiving warm love from a committed teacher. In this setting, you are free to include Bible stories and other religious books among the materials, to teach the children songs of praise, to talk about God, to pray before the morning juice and crackers, to have services of worship, and to teach about the meaning of Christmas and Easter. Some churches have worked out an arrangement whereby the professional teacher or one of the helpers also teaches on Sunday morning, thereby preserving a continuity with those among the parish children who attend the weekday group.

The day nursery, day-care center, and Head Start

program are other weekday educational uses of your building. You would probably sponsor such a program rather than establish it, for state or federal money is involved and the religious teaching possible in your own program cannot be included. It is, however, a form of Christian witness. In offering the use of your building (for which you are paid) you are saying that as a parish you are concerned about the need some children have for the kind of program Head Start or day nursery can give as an important part of their development. You are expressing your concern for parents and their children. Day care can assure the child security during whatever hours the parents are working.

It is a sad thing that some church buildings remain empty all week while such needs exist within a community. No church need be anxious about what would happen to the building if it were used so much, although the house committee is understandably concerned in this matter. You will probably find that those who use the building also have a sense of responsibility—at least you must trust them until you learn otherwise. Remember that buildings, like people, are meant to spend their lives for some good purpose.

After-school programs are another possibility. These have several advantages. The children have come from a school program and will expect a serious learning experience. They are in everyday clothes, work clothes, so to speak. They are in the community because school attendance is required (however often they may be away weekends). You may find it easier to get some teachers who would not be available on Sunday morning.

Each point is balanced by a disadvantage. After being in school all day, children may desire nothing less than to go back to school. Try as you may to clear the calendar with the schools so that churches are left one free afternoon for their activities, parents will rush in to fill the time with music, dental, or other appointments. Few working men or women will be available for teaching. High school students will probably be unavailable because their school day tends to be long.

However, weekday programs of one kind or another have been going on for half a century. Sometimes they are run by a single parish; some are cooperative ventures. A number of curricular materials are published for just that purpose. The Catholic church for a long time has had the CCD program in which teachers hold a weekly session for the children who do not go to parochial schools. Some people have welcomed released time because it guarantees them a time slot, however small, in the child's week. When, however, this slot is the last hour of the day and the same hour all over a city, many churches are hard put to find teachers adequate to sustain a program of excellence. The kind of released-time program which varies the day from grade to grade and from school to school makes possible a professionally staffed program. In these situations, it can be an interdenominational approach. It also makes fuller use of church facilities. This works best if there is a church building near the school from which the children are being released. A few well-funded programs brought mobile classrooms, which a professional teacher took from school to school, making an instant environment for teaching.

Special Occasions

You should not feel that a weekday program must be continued for an entire year. Some successful ones have been short-term sessions: four weeks in December in a getting-ready-for-Christmas teaching unit or a Lenten weekday study program. Special times like these encourage participation to a larger extent than might be possible at other times.

Some after-school activities have been running for a long time. Children's choirs usually meet at this time. Choir practice can be combined with a study and activity program, ending with supper or beginning with an afternoon snack.

Confirmation or church membership programs have frequently been scheduled for weekdays because when the children go directly from school to church there can be a solid time for work and regular attendance can be expected. Occasionally a continuing weekday program has grown out of such a beginning. The Lutheran church has a three-year confirmation program and when this is scheduled for a weekday afternoon, it can establish a pattern.

The confirmation program is frequently carried out on Saturday morning. This permits a two-and-a-half-hour program with several kinds of activities: worship, study and research, and discussion and action. Field trips or a long session with a resource person are possible. A full-length film could be shown. An able teacher would rejoice in such a block of time. However (all good possibilities have drawbacks), the Sunday School which has difficulties with attendance on Sunday is not going to find many more families available on Saturday. This is the day for sleeping late, doing house chores, and engaging in recreational activities. Nevertheless, the Saturday School cannot be completely dismissed until you have surveyed the time possibilities.

Then there is the evening. You are already using this for young people's events, adult study groups, lectures, discussions, couples' groups, and church suppers. Remember that these events are Christian education activities. Where church suppers are a custom (especially where each family brings a dish, thus simplifying the work), this is a wonderful opportunity for fellowship, worship, and study. Begin early. Have one main event: Bible presentation (your pastor should be able to do that one), a speaker, film, music—you will think of other possibilities. Sometimes you will want to break into small groups to talk about what has been heard and seen. Sometimes you will find it a rich experience to form intergenerational groups. Sometimes you will want separate groups for children, youth, and adults.

One parish sustained this kind of program as their only educational one for a year. They met each week from September through May, planning six-week study units and taking a break at Christmas and Easter. Most of you will find it more practical as an auxiliary program either on a monthly basis or concentrated at a particular time of year, such as Lent. In places where people tend to stay at home during the summer, this might offer a relaxed weekly activity. The evening setup has the advantage of bringing the whole family together and of making available a reasonable block of time in which to work out meaningful learning. Fellowship, worship, and study become an integral experience and you are truly a church family.

Consider the possibility of a one-day event. I have known churches to develop an all-day children's program for a weekday school holiday.

Saturday is useful for leadership training. Admittedly this requires the cooperation of some member of the family to care for the household while another member attends the sessions. If you begin in the morning, have lunch together, and end by mid-afternoon, you will have a solid block of time for working together. Add a Friday evening session and a full study unit can be developed on any subject.

Events

Church councils could use such a block of time on a Saturday or Sunday to plan their work at the beginning of the year and another later to evaluate it. Leave immediately after the morning service, have lunch together, and work through the afternoon and evening. This could be held in your church building, but there is a particular value in going elsewhere if you are fortunate enough to have a conveniently located conference center, a member's vacation house, or even another church. The purpose will determine the setting. If you need to look at your resources, then you will want to meet on the premises. Your best depth thinking, however, will be done if you go a distance. There are many ways of developing a program when you are not confined to one or two hours. Try it and see.

This is the time to mention retreats, a special kind of learning experience. Nothing can replace the prayer group whose members meet regularly week after week, but the longer time occasionally set aside, brings its own spiritual fruitfulness. One day of quiet meditations and waiting on God can be an invaluable source of strength.

How about a family day? Having fun together is an educational experience, too. The church picnic is newly popular because people like to be informal. (Some people dislike all picnics, but there are variations to suit almost anyone.) I have known families with a home at the shore or rolling acres of farmland who invited the parish to share these pleasures for a day. It isn't a Sunday School experience but there couldn't be a better way of supplementing what the Sunday School is trying to do. Imagine how many parents and teachers could get together at such an event!

The field trip should be mentioned as another form of an all-day event. I remember a city church in which a Saturday tour was planned to visit church-related agencies in the area. It was surprising how many there were: a nursery school, a neighborhood center, a boys' school, and a hospital program. This was a real learning experience. The people working in these agencies were able to explain to us on the spot how their Christian witness was taking place and could urge more participation by our congregation.

Young people have carried this idea further, taking weekend field trips by bus. A variant is the work-camp experience which may last from a week to a month or more and be carried on in any place where the church's mission can use their help while they observe firsthand the need for dedicated service. Young people have gone to many places—Alaska, the Caribbean, Europe, and other parts of the world.

Young people find a weekend experience a time for fellowship, learning, and a deepening of the spiritual life. For younger adolescents, you may wish to begin on a Friday evening and end with Saturday lunch, holding only two sessions. Progress from that brief experience to one which begins with Friday dinner and goes through Saturday afternoon. A full Friday to Sunday weekend is best for seasoned conference goers. It provides a wealth of opportunities for really digging into an area of study and for experiencing Christian living and worship on a deep level. You will find many materials to help with content and methods on specific themes.

Summary

The types of teaching:

1. Sunday
   morning: before or after morning worship integrated with the morning service
   evening: young people's group, adult study
2. Weekdays
   morning: for preschoolers and mothers, day care centers, church nursery school and kindergarten, Head Start program
   after school: weekday study programs, released-time classes, choir, confirmation class, short-term study groups
   evening (or late afternoon into evening): junior high programs, high school groups, family supper/study events, adult groups
3. Saturday: confirmation class, Saturday School, day long event for children, families, teachers, and leadership training, field trips
4. Overnight or weekend: young people's conferences or retreats, adult planning conferences, or retreats, and family camping
5. Summer: vacation church school, day camping, overnight camping (including work camps), and conferences

8
Youth Likes to Be Different

You do not need to be told that young people are an important part of the Sunday School. They are not the church of the future; they are the young church right now. No longer children, they do not want to be treated like "the rest of the Sunday School." What does this mean?

First think of the kind of people who would make good teachers and leaders for adolescents. It goes without saying that these must be people with whom the young people can feel comfortable, knowing that they are liked and appreciated for being themselves. They do not have to be anxious about making mistakes, and the growing pains of the young are understood.

Needs of Young People

Adolescents need an opportunity to be together both in a large group and in small groups according to needs. There is a security in the large group which seems to comfort the young. This is why rallies are popular, whether rock festivals or Young Life crusades. You will want to plan opportunities where there will be events to include all young people. If you are too small a congregation to have a fairly large group, consider a cooperative relationship with one or more churches in the area. You can alternate between meeting together and in separate, small groups.

There is also the need for intimacy, for being part of a group small enough to know each other and be known. This can be accomplished through home gatherings, committee work, special projects, small group discussions, or prayer groups. The focus of the groups becomes clear as the young people make their needs known to understanding leaders and to members of their own steering committee.

The size of groups suggests the kinds of environment the young people will need. They have to fit into existent space structures, but everyone will be more content if an effort is made to find the kind of space through which their needs can be comfortably met rather than the other way around. If you need a small room and there is none available in the church building, try meeting in homes. If a meal is planned, hopefully the adults (usually meaning the women) will show the young people how to use the kitchen and keep it clean. The adult leaders and youth representatives could meet with the house or housekeeping committee and promise that the group will use the kitchen responsibly.

This is mentioned because tension sometimes arises in a church between young people and adults over issues concerning the use of rooms. Adults feel the facilities are easily misused; the young people feel they are neither trusted nor wanted. Someone needs the skill to encourage the kind of communication through which the experience of Christian fellowship can be made real.

Young people usually want to *create* their own environment. In their changing fashions and emphases, it would be difficult for adults to decide the best decor. The coffee house atmosphere was popular for awhile. What is the successor? Most young people's groups will still have to use the setting they find, multipurpose rooms which you hope will suit the nature of their program.

Some churches have found that the Sunday morning youth program wavers. Saturday night is important in their social life, and they will get up for a morning program only if it is vital to them. This is a challenge, but if you cannot meet it, there is no cause for discouragement. Varying times for teaching applies as much to young people as to any other group. Check again the list at the end of chapter 7 to see how many of the occasions specifically mention possible use by youth.

The really important time for them is morning worship. As part of the congregation they indicate that they have become adult Christians. Young people who gladly go to their own group meeting but are absent here, have not understood one part of their commitment to Christ. Encouraging church attendance among the young is at least as much a task of the Sunday School as is promoting the development of a high school class.

Times for Meeting

Whatever time the younger Sunday School groups meet, the older youth should not be bound by that time for their classes. Many have a high degree of mobility and—whether we like it or not—prefer to attend church events with friends rather than with family. Yet, I am serious about the need for the church to incorporate this age group. A Sunday School that has only children in attendance is severely limited in what it can do. Episcopal Sunday School attendance has been curtailed when children are confirmed at an early age and tend to drop out at this point. Lutheran churches have tried to reverse the trend by having a three-year confirmation training for grades seven through nine. Other denominations seem less affected by the relationship between the age of commitment and attendance at Sunday School. We need to get away from the idea that Sunday School is for children. Adolescents are the *bridge* generation who can keep a solid sense of continuing learning alive. They are the elder members, and junior highs especially take their cues from older peers.

So when the adolescents are attending morning worship, you will next want to find with them the best time for their group meeting. Some prefer to meet after the church service. Adult groups frequently choose this time and adolescents would prefer to meet when adults do rather than at the time the children meet. The Sunday morning group is usually a discussion, study, and research session. Many curricular materials stress life-experience units for adolescents. One of the most popular young people's materials begins with Bible study and asks in a searching way "What does this say to me?"

Young people want to be leaders in their group, but they also want the support of adult leaders. They want to talk about the concerns of their own lives, but they have come to realize that the Bible has some answers they can't find elsewhere. Yet how few adolescents really know how to use the tools of Bible study! They are accustomed to research in school, but we have not often made available to them the concordances, dictionaries, and commentaries that would help them to better understand the word of God in Scripture.

So if Sunday School is meant as a study program, it may take place on Sunday morning, but if there is no room that the young people can call their own during the regular hour, consider scheduling their meeting (as well as that of the adults) at a different time. You might even invite older adolescents to join adult programs. They might find such groups seriously concerned with their kind of issues, and their sharp minds might be a stimulus to the adults in the class.

It has been customary to assume that high school students will meet for two sessions: morning and evening. Do not consider this essential. Do not assume that there must be a group meeting every Sunday evening. High school today is very demanding. Family weekend activities may limit the possibilities of evening groups. Sometimes we can become so insistent on continuing a long-held pattern as to forget that the quality of the program is what really counts. Moreover, although you want to meet the needs of as many of your young people as possible, accept the fact that not everyone will be interested in joining a group. So perhaps instead of dreaming of an all-encompassing youth group, some churches should think of several options, as they do in planning for adults: a prayer group, small Bible study groups, a faith-sharing group, or a project or service group. Others would like to learn more about essentials of the Christian faith—especially older adolescents whose courses at school bring them a knowledge of world culture, psychology, and philosophy.

Working and Growing

Young people enjoy activity. They are impatient with people who only talk. They want to express their faith. One

Christian growth. Remember that some among these young people are being called into full-time Christian service.

Work projects are another form of action which appeals to young people. The obvious ones are the money-making projects: ways of finding money for their group and forms of participation in church events. You know the possibilities. The annual fair, summer or winter, is part of the life of many churches in which young people happily participate. Some will help in the arduous work of setting up rooms. They may want to have their own sales project. Traditionally they have waited on tables at a dinner, and if you serve buffet style, they are needed to keep things moving smoothly.

Their music is lovely and they sing with an easy informality that brings warmth and joy. Let them use these gifts in informal ways at church events (singing minstrels during the fair or at a meal). Encourage them to join the choir. If you are a large congregation, develop a youth choir. The quality of music performed by community groups indicates talents frequently neglected in church life. I knew a parish whose annual meeting was enriched through a group of high school singers whose performance made a transition between the fellowship dinner and the annual reports.

Building projects are another form of action. Do you include the young people when there are painting and other refurbishing projects? Invite their ideas as well as their labor. It has been a custom to permit the young people to fix up a room of their own when such was available. Be sure this is granted generously and not as a way of keeping them by themselves. They are part of the whole fellowhip and the building belongs to everyone. Remember that they will remain longest with whatever changes are made—unless you assume that most young people will leave the community when they reach adulthood. Whenever volunteer labor is use of their talents has always been with children in the Sunday School. This has had good results. Many adolescents have a naturally easy way with children. They are the most loved baby-sitters, and so it is not surprising that their talent should be requested in the Sunday School. Nothing upsets them. They have encouraging words for the quiet child, while a diverting suggestion calms the difficult one. There is no reason for a teacher to be without helpers when there are high school students available.

But please give them opportunities to grow. Remember that they will become the next generation of teachers. Do not keep them running errands, taking attendance, finding supplies, and monitoring the edges of the story circle. Let the young helper tell the story, teach songs, or plan an activity. Vary the assignments according to the helper's abilities. Children need older boys and girls as examples.

Every teacher admits to learning a great deal through teaching others. Preparation for class is a strong motivation for learning; so helping to teach children is a good way for high school young people to learn more about their own faith.

Teaching, you will say, takes young people from their own class. Yes, if you insist that all must go to one class which meets when the rest of the Sunday School meets. If you can view high school helpers as being a class, remember the learning which comes through their attendance at teacher training meetings. A large Sunday School might have an occasional gathering specifically for the high school teaching assistants so that they can talk about their work, their needs, and their place as helpers in the Sunday School. Some may feel that they are being ordered around; others may long to be in charge of a class. You need to know this so that the experience can become a satisfying part of their own used for performing professional work, the church as a corporate body takes responsibility for the safety of all workers. Check on this: parental permission may be required for those under eighteen years old.

Special Projects

Community work projects have enlisted the enthusiasm of young people in recent years. Older young people especially have shared their social concerns through involvement. There are few places where they can express their Christian witness, but adult Christians as prime movers in community agencies and groups can help develop such opportunities. Some high schools have a liaison with the wider community and are sensitive to this kind of learning activity. The church cannot do less for we profess to bring Christ to the world and to be as Christ in the world.

Field trips are another possibility for learning. This has already been outlined under the heading "Events" (chapter 7) and need not be elaborated here. Some forms of field trips are especially useful for expressing adolescent concern. It is important that careful preparation be made whether for a day, weekend, or longer excursion. The young people should become involved in planning the event, getting acquainted with people they will later meet as they make initial contacts by telephone or letter. They can share reading and research on the history, present situation, and needs of people and places. They can talk with nearby people who have information.

The follow-up action after their return is also important: to share with one another the differences between their expectations and what they found; to reflect on what they learned; and to ask what further they need to learn or to do.

The field trip is not easy to plan. It requires dedicated, skilled adult leaders and parents willing to give their time to help. The reward, however, can be great through the deepened understanding which comes from a live experience.

While talking about the possibility of an extended learning experience another opportunity should be mentioned from chapter 7—the overnight or weekend conference or retreat. There is a difference; each has its own value.

A conference is a concentrated way of looking at an area of inquiry, using a variety of methods to help participants think deeply and form new understandings. A retreat is a way of heightening the awareness of the presence of God among his people and within each retreatant as a person. This interaction with God—sometimes alone, at other times participating in group prayer—gives depth to the retreat experience. Scripture, for example, could be the subject of either a conference or a retreat. During a conference, you might study one book, or idea, reading a section and researching the background by learning from films, work books, or a study course. Finally a passage could be devotionally studied by asking questions, such as what the text said to those for whom it was first written and what it says to each one now. In a retreat, however, only the last question is really the subject. You might concentrate on only one passage or on a specific passage for each session. There would be a meditation by a leader and sharing ideas with one another in small groups.

There would also be worship—together and alone. A retreat is for spiritual renewal. It is suggested because young people have become aware of a need for a deeper spiritual life and some have turned from the Christian way. They have found a sense of the transcendent through Zen exercises or Hindu forms of meditation. Some have found a vital faith through the Jesus movement. Few have ever heard about the

Christian devotional tradition: the desert fathers in the third century, the monastic orders, the great mystics of the Middle Ages, the tradition and witness of the Society of Friends, or the shared prayer of mutual strengthening among small religious groups of the pietist heritage. Can this be recovered for our young people? It belongs to us all.

Recognition

Young people like recognition and receive little from the church. One Sunday of recognition, called Youth Sunday because they conduct the morning service, can be an uncomfortable experience as they are asked to perform unaccustomed actions. Better to invite their participation on other Sundays as readers or in the choir. They need to be on church committees in sufficient numbers so that they do not feel overwhelmed by older adults. One adolescent on a committee of adults can feel isolated. When this happens, their inclusion on church committees becomes only a gesture. Do we want it this way, or do we really want their contributions? Perhaps they could be co-opted members without vote in order that their views might be heard.

Another possibility is to encourage young committee members to caucus together and to share with their young people's group the inner workings of the parish machinery.

Young people today are looking for ways of commitment. We have encouraged them to commit their lives to Jesus Christ as their Lord and Savior. How have we upheld them in this commitment? Have adults been sufficiently committed so that young people feel strengthened by the power of the Holy Spirit manifested within the whole congregation? Are they given tasks in the life of the church through which to express their commitment? Are they encouraged as they try to witness to their faith in everyday life? Is the example of adult members an encouragement?

Everyone can become involved in some way in the life of the church. It should not be expected that every teenager will be doing everything. Be concerned enough about them to have many available avenues and to encourage each to find a place: in Sunday morning class, as a Sunday School worker, attending morning worship (a must), in an evening group, at work within the life of the parish, through special projects, field trips, conferences, or retreats, in community work or on church committees.

Summary

1. Youth like to have programs: morning or evening.
2. Youth like to do things: helping in the Sunday School, work projects, field trips, and conferences or retreats.
3. Youth like recognition as adults: in choir membership and church committees.
4. Youth are looking for commitment.

9

Adults Are in the Picture

If you have a strong Sunday School, the chances are that a strong adult group is part of it. If you have a weak one, it is likely that there is no adult group, a struggling high school group, and a junior high group that is alternately large or small, depending on its leadership. Obviously adult education is a key to a totally strong program.

The Adult Class

There have been times and places when an adult Sunday School class almost seemed to be the church. It gathered in numbers rivaling those at morning worship. The class session opened with a worship service so complete that some members felt no need for any other. The leader taught by the lecture method, usually an exegetical and expository study of the Bible. There were churches in which Sunday School superintendents, desperate for teachers, murmured that able-bodied adults who had been learning about Scripture for years in their class well might try to teach it to others. But on the whole, its very presence was a strength to the total structure. The excesses of such a class can be overcome in several ways.

It needs to be consciously a member of the whole Sunday School enterprise. Its leaders should attend teachers' meetings (exposure to a variety of teaching methods could be helpful). Its money should be part of the total Sunday School offering which in turn should be part of the church budget. The curriculum, when still using the international lesson outlines, can be enriched by having available to leaders several of the new commentaries published each year instead of using only one. Some adult groups are ready to move into more flexible directions such as the occasional use of smaller study units, development ofrotating class leaders, encouragement of wider participation in raising questions and sharing responses. Although many people like to feel that they belong to a large group, some hestitate to speak out in such a group, and so the class becomes a listening situation rather than a sharing one.

The possibilities for adult Sunday School groups are so extensive and so varied that the needs of any church can be met. No established group needs to be threatened if other groups are formed, even if some of their members join the new group. No one who wants a different group should feel that the established one is a hindrance to the new group's formation. What possibilities are there?

The first consideration has to do with subject. If one group is built around biblical study, how about forming another concerned with the meaning of faith: prayer, understanding God, the work of the Holy Spirit, the meaning of Christ for us, being part of the church? Some would find it helpful to study the meaning of the Christian experience in daily life. Recently, publishers have been printing study guides to accompany new books with a wide circulation. Bringing Christian insights to bear on important books is an excellent extension of the concern to interpret the faith. Another concern is that of understanding persons: why they act as they do, their interrelationships with one another, or the religious development of children. Teachers and parents are particularly interested in such areas. The mission of the church is important: the evangelistic concern at home and abroad, our relationship with other religious faiths, and our understanding of other religions. The lists of publishers of religious books will furnish you with useful titles in paperbound.

The second possibility has to do with format. Some people learn best in a large group in which a knowledgeable person makes a presentation. Some may think this is passive learning; the student is a sponge to soak up information without giving any response. If some people prefer this way, there is no reason to change it. Others want to do some of the talking themselves, to ask questions and make comments. While even a large group can make time for this, few adults are brave enough to ask questions in such a setting. They need to be in a small group where people know one another in order to have confidence to speak. This gives class members an opportunity to address one another, and the result can be a lively conversation and discussion. Remember that not everyone is comfortable leading this kind of group. Some teachers have to feel that they are in control of the class (in a good way, of course). They do the talking and answer the questions.

Others enjoy the flow of discussion and the variety of viewpoints. They see their job as keeping the ball rolling, helping class members to listen to one another and to respect one another's opinions and statements. In such a group, it is not important that there be one final agreed-upon conclusion, although a general summary may be made orally with contributions from volunteers. Sometimes one person is asked to keep notes during the session.

Exploring Methods

In other learning settings, a wide variety of methods may be used. A resource person, knowledgeable in a specific subject, could make a presentation (sometimes illustrated) and respond at length to questions asked by the group. Frequently, this will be in an area in which the class has done some preparatory research and has some definite ideas of what they wish to learn from the visitor. A panel discussion can be a fruitful source of sharing. I was recently in a group in which the subject under discussion was the meaning of the Christian emphasis on *simplicity of life*. Three members opened the session by sharing their understanding: an older person, someone in middle age, and a young adult. What a breadth of experience in the Christian life they represented! It was a wonderful beginning to open up the area for everyone present.

The use of audio-visual materials is widespread. You will find that filmstrip and film are designed to be used quite differently (apart from the fact that there is a vast difference in cost). A filmstrip gives information. It is excellent for presenting a situation or describing visually how to do something. But a filmstrip has rarely been adequate for setting a mood. Only now are we beginning to get the kind of filmstrip which has emotional impact. A carousel projector plus a soundtrack with vivid, emotionally laden sounds, music, and words is the key to this kind of presentation.

Films continue to grow shorter. Consider the one-minute "spots" which can leave the viewer thoughtful before the discussion begins. No further introduction is needed. There are five- and ten-minute films with profound impact. A fifteen- to thirty-minute film can open up all kinds of questions. Happy the group whose leader first lets the film speak for itself, quietly standing aside after viewing it so that all who wish may share their insights. It is amazing the differences which appear, the little touches which one person sees or another remembers. Finally something akin to the director's intention begins to emerge. Then you are ready to ask other questions—not simply what do you see, or what do you think the director is trying to say—but what does it mean, and what is your critique of its meaning in terms of Christian faith and in terms of your life?

Cassettes are becoming increasingly useful. The voices of people we could never hope to hear in person are made available to groups through this medium. Be sure that you have a quality machine for playback so that the tone is good and the voices clear. It is not as easy to listen to a disembodied voice as it is to hear a speaker standing before you. One isn't quite sure where to focus attention. Cassettes are best used for a small group. The leader should become thoroughly familiar with the information in order to anticipate responses and be prepared with questions. After listening, it may be necessary first to recapitulate the essence of the material so that you are sure everyone has heard similar words. (You might also have chosen to outline the main points on a chalkboard before the session began.) Then you are ready to discuss it as a group. Cassettes are now available on many subjects, including whole series for teacher training and the training of other church leaders.

Games are another of the newer media, and some are prepared for use with large groups. Many, however, can be played only in a group of twelve to sixteen and should be thought of for your smaller classes. These too cover many subjects: understanding problem areas in church and society, teacher training, or learning biblical material. Some games may seem expensive but when they can be reused, they are a resource to consider.

Times for Learning

Adult Sunday School classes may be developed, not only on the basis of subject or method, but also in terms of people with a common interest. Parents form a natural learning group. It is good for a couple to study together and not only about the religious nurture of children. If they study the Bible together, they have a mutual basis on which to share their insights. By deepening their faith, they become more able to communicate faith to children.

There are convenient times for teaching when non-working mothers are available—mornings, for example. They can form a group to discuss the bearing of the biblical faith on those things which are of primary concern to them. Mornings are the most convenient time although it must not be assumed that all mothers are free in the morning.

We do not always think of the organized groups in our churches as educational groups, but they are. To begin with, a person learns through every activity. What are the adults in your church learning through their groups? I know women who are learning a happy sense of fellowship and a real feeling of being useful as they meet together to work on bazaar projects. There are others who get the impression that the only church work women do is to raise money. There should be room for those who want to study the Bible together, to grow in the life of prayer, to express their experiences from the working world or community affairs to which they give so much voluntary time. Do you have a couples group, and is it primarily for social purposes? In some churches, younger couples are a minority group and the fellowship they find in coming together is important in making the church a part of their lives. They might also be interested in using some of the methods suggested earlier—especially film, games, or a resource speaker.

What do you do at all-church meetings? The church supper is still a vital part of the fellowship of many churches. What an opportunity for learning together! When you stop to think of it, the potluck supper really links us with the first years of the life of the Christian community when all brought and shared the food as they met, ate, and worshipped together. Would that our church suppers could always be such love feasts! Of course, you worship together at such times either around the tables or in the church. Church suppers are a wonderful time for singing together and for learning hymns. What kind of a learning program will you have? Film will be one form. Don't forget the wonderful free resources from denominational film libraries and your state or city public library. Speakers are another resource to consider. If you are having a series of suppers (one always thinks of the traditional Lenten weeks) people might be ready for the seriousness of biblical study. What a wonderful experience that could be: after the leader presents a theme and a passage, the people gathered around each table could share insights. What was the writer saying to his contemporaries? What is the passage saying to us? At the conclusion, someone from each group could share thoughts briefly and simply with the rest. God can speak to his people gathered together to learn from his Holy Word.

We seldom realize that the official groups which govern our churches are possible teaching groups, but they can be.

Does your governing board spend all its time on the immediate concerns of the month? That would be too bad. They could look at their task more broadly and thereby be taking it more seriously. What really are they trying to do? There are pertinent Scripture passages for study which might give them insights.

Special Activities

Choir is another of the adult activities through which learning is taking place. Basically, choir members are learning through the music they sing; so it is important to choose hymns carefully and to study the meaning of words as they learn to sing them. What is the anthem really saying? Are these ideas faithful to the biblical message and to the meaning of the Christian faith or are they sweet and sentimental? Great music has been written throughout all the centuries of the church's life; so be sure that your choir has an opportunity to use appropriate selections.

Popular church music has a place as an important part of our heritage: it is a special way of expressing to one another what the faith means to us. Gospel hymns are part of this heritage. The best hymns have not yet been selected by the process of time; so some that we have are not as useful as they should be. Choose carefully. Learning *about* hymns is an important part of learning how to sing them. Not every choir leader is equal to this kind of teaching. Happy those who are for their choir members will have a deeper understanding of the words they sing.

Don't overlook the use of good recordings for teaching. People can learn simply by listening to that which is beautiful, and there is a great heritage of religious music on records.

Remember that training events are part of the religious education of adults. The many possibilities for teacher training suggested in chapter 2 and ways in which church committees are training for their jobs should also be counted. Family events are outlined in chapter 4. These adult education events are of special importance because they span the generations.

Some parishes have the custom of a coffee hour after the morning service. The chief value is for people to get to know one another and for newcomers to be warmly welcomed. These things do not just happen. Some people have to be specially delegated to encourage getting acquainted. Coffee hour can also become a teaching opportunity. People take their cups to tables and begin their Bible study. I have known a small group to read Mark's Gospel and the Book of the Acts this way. Use a popular translation like *Living Bible* or *Good News for Modern Man*.

Finally, the adults in your church should be involved in the wider community of faith. This might mean studying with people from other churches in the neighborhood or others from your own denominational group. It would certainly include involvement in area groups as leaders, committee members, or attendants. What they learn can be brought home and shared with others of the congregation. Probably the most honored responsibility which can come to any member is to be appointed or elected an official delegate to a national denominational convention. This calls for study of preliminary papers, a sifting of the issues, and prayerful preparation with others in the congregation. This too is an area of witness.

Summary

Adult educational events:

1. The adult Sunday School class
2. Informal groups
3. Morning groups for nonworking women
4. All-church events
5. Varieties of evening groups
6. Training events for teachers, officers, and committee members
7. Community, ecumenical, or denominational events

10
We Worship Together

Christian worship has always been a way of Christian teaching. The book of the Acts reports that the first Christians gathered together for prayer, fellowship, and teaching. The Scriptures were read at worship. The writings were not in every household as the Bible is today, although wealthy families owned the parchment books just coming into use. The scrolls used in a synagogue were valuable, historic treasures.

Remembrances of Jesus—his words and works, the stories he told, and the teachings he gave—were circulated at these gatherings either by word of mouth or in written collections. Paul's letters indicate traditions handed on to him by the apostles as well as revelations he had himself received from the Lord. (Recall that the words of Jesus, "It is more blessed to give than to receive," are preserved through the writings of Paul.)

The Lord's Supper was observed among the congregations as a memorial, an assurance of the immediate presence of the Lord and the promise of his return. Some of the hymns sung at worship have come to us through the pages of the New Testament. Such songs are expressions of praise and prayer and affirmations of faith—a real avenue for learning. Prayer in the congregation was another way by which new Christians learned for whom and for what to pray.

Learning through Worship

All of this is equally true today. New Christians and children growing up in the household of faith learn about their faith through listening to and taking part in the hymns, Scripture, sermon, and prayer. This is why any congregation has to be careful that the hymns used really express what they believe to be true about the biblical faith and that full use is made of the reading of Scripture in the service. Some churches regularly have three lessons: one each from the Old Testament, Epistle, and Gospel. The Psalms have always been used in Christian worship.

People learn by doing; so the very fact of being present at Sunday worship is part of learning. One feels joy and thanksgiving by singing hymns of praise. One learns how to pray in thanksgiving, contrition, intercession, and petition because one is doing this as part of a congregation. A person begins to understand Scripture by listening carefully while passages are read and explained week by week. The Lord's Supper becomes vivid because one is part of a congregation remembering through the breaking of bread together.

People also learn as they study the materials they are using. There are some congregations in which groups meet each week to study biblical passages that will be read on Sunday morning. They are really prepared to listen to the sermon, and the minister preparing for Sunday is aware that others also are seeking to understand more deeply the Word of God. Each person might study the Scripture reading during the week following the service.

Some churches make it a practice to teach new hymns. This helps people to look at the meaning of the words and to see how the music expresses that meaning. Church suppers provide further occasions for learning new hymns. A Bible study group would be amazed to discover how many hymns are directly inspired by words of Scripture, not only from the Psalms, but from allusions to people, places, and teachings. Prayer groups, through their practice of prayer, help members to become more aware of their place in the congregation at worship.

If you wonder what this has to do with Sunday School, the answer is that the Sunday School needs to be aware of other places where learning is taking place. In chapter 2, mention was made of churches in which the whole family attends the morning service together, children remaining there for part or all of the time, depending on the occasion. The child who worships with the whole congregation is learning. Much of the content will escape the very young, but the most important part—absorbing the meaning of what it means to pray, praise, listen, and feel part of a worshipping community—is there. This is true in a particular way when the child attends with a parent. It can also happen when other members of the congregation make all children feel at home.

Helping Children Worship

Try to find ways of helping parents interpret the service to their children. If yours is a parish in which the Scripture lessons and hymns are planned in advance, then you can give specific suggestions. The newsletter or Sunday bulletin can give such information. A parents' meeting could encourage the practice.

General suggestions can be used informally to encourage spontaneous reflection. Parents could focus on one hymn. What did you most enjoy singing today? What were the words saying? (Parents might make note of difficult words.) Can you hum the tune? (It would be a good idea for each family to own a copy of the hymnal.) What is the Scripture about and what is the teaching or story? What is God saying to humanity? What is he saying to us? What do the words mean to you? What did the minister say about this in the sermon? The conversation could end with simple prayers of thanksgiving and petition with each participating. This kind of family gathering offers parents a simple way of taking part directly in their children's Christian nurture. Sharing faith in the family is important.

Sunday School is another place for reflecting on what the worship service means. When Sunday School meets before the church service, teachers could make a point of preparing the children: reminding them of why we go to church, how we act, what to expect from being there, and how to listen. Invite questions and share experiences from being in church. When children go to classes after attending the service, teachers and children can recall what they have been hearing and doing. This is a good time to pick up misunderstandings which come when children do not hear a pronunciation correctly or misunderstand the meaning of words.

Beyond reflection on the service, the Sunday School class can be a place to learn and prepare for attendance at church. The direct use of the Bible in class is important. Passages used will become familiar when heard in the service. Verses heard will cause even a young child to respond with recognition, as if to say "I know that." Familiar stories are heard in biblical language. Familiar psalms are read as responsive readings. Incidentally, it is helpful to read psalms responsively in class, both as a way of learning how to read them and as a way of becoming familiar with the psalms themselves. Some teachers arrange the psalms for choric reading, yet another use.

Then there are hymns. Some with simple words and tune are composed just for children. But the regular hymnal contains songs with easily learned rhythms and enough repetition of words so that children can understand them. After all, most adults in church are not skilled singers. Hopefully they are enthusiastic ones! This is how you want the children to be. People feel comfortable with music with which they are familiar. This means that repetition is good, if not carried too far. It is important to introduce a new hymn occasionally and use it until it becomes familiar. Teachers can become alert to what is being sung in the church service and find ways of using these hymns in class. Don't forget that you can also use the words of hymns as teaching material. You will find them good illustrations. The words of some hymns are beautiful prayers and could be used in unison at the opening or close of a session.

Sunday School Worship

Your immediate concern is the Sunday School worship service. Some of you bring the whole group together so that the younger members learn from the older ones. When you do this, it is important that there be something for everyone. Even the youngest member present needs to understand what is going on. Some of us can still remember opening exercises which to our young minds and bodies seemed to go on forever.

Opening worship for the adult class runs the risk of being a brief repetition of the morning service. Avoid this! It will tempt some members to feel that they have been to church, so why go again? You are so used to the form of the regular service that it may be difficult to think about other possibilities.

Make this service brief. What is your purpose in having one to begin with? It is to bring you together as a class in the presence of God that you may be aware of the guidance of this Holy Spirit as you search the Scriptures together. When you use a hymn, let it be one which turns your attention to your purpose or one which highlights the theme of the day's lesson. You might use the Scripture passage which you will be studying. It is good to hear it read devotionally before you begin to study the words. You may not wish to have any message because the lesson itself is the message, or you may wish to have a brief, two-minute commentary on what essentially the passage is saying. Any words spoken in the opening worship of the adult class should avoid being either a substitute for the sermon or a repetition of the class session. Use your own judgment.

Prayer is the most important part of your opening worship, because when you are serious about wanting to know the meaning of Scripture, you will be serious about asking God's guidance as you do so. If there is any sense of fellowship in the group, this will also be the time when you bring before God intercessions for one another, needs and thanksgivings for those present and those absent.

Whether this opening service is *formal* or *informal*—whatever those terms may mean in your church—is entirely a matter of the general practices within your congregation. Some congregations (and whole denominations) are most comfortable with worship within a formal setting. The order of worship does not change and a leader is responsible for the whole. Others are more at ease with a looser structure: hymns may be chosen on the spot, prayer be invited from among the group, and comment on Scripture is open to all. Just be sure the timing does not get out of hand. Keep it short, whatever you do!

Children's Worship

Children's worship should be planned by teachers who understand children and who appreciate their growth in faith. Informality and flexibility are the keynotes, even when you have a carefully ordered service. You say this is a contradiction? Not at all. Children like to know the order in which things are going to happen. School is arranged this way. At home they know the times for play, meals, and going to bed. This gives them a sense of security. They like to know whether you are going to begin with a gathering for worship or end with it. You would not have to follow one schedule week after week. Just don't switch every week.

Children also like to have some idea of a rhythm for the service. Do you gather in one spot? Do you sit on the floor in a circle or on chairs or in rows? Is there some focus of interest, such as a table with a Bible on it? Do you begin with a hymn or with quiet words of invitation to worship—"I was glad when they said to me: let us go to the house of the Lord."

Use joyous hymns: hymns of praise and thanksgiving. Use quiet hymns expressing the assurance of God's love and care, his forgiveness and help. Avoid preachy hymns that tell children how to act. They can learn manners at home. As was said earlier, hymns have always been a way through which Christians at worship expressed their praise and adoration in the presence of God. Let the children feel this from their earliest experiences. They can learn a wide variety of tunes; so try a few carefully selected from the congregational hymnal. You will find that the refrain to a hymn is especially enjoyed.

Prayer is the heart of the children's worship. For many this will be an introduction to praying with others. Not all children experience family prayer at home. In Sunday School, the faith of the teacher shines through to the children. They know whether belief is a matter of words or the expression of a relationship to the living God. Many children have had their own love for Christ quickened by the faith of a Sunday School teacher. No further prescription need be given. By your example and encouragement, teach the child to feel joyous and loving in the presence of God, to express thanksgiving for the gifts given, and to ask trustingly (and trust is natural to a child) for help, reassurance, and forgiveness.

Biblical stories and verses, as well as your own experience, will encourage the children in prayer. Be sure to give them opportunity to participate. With the youngest ones, you may wish to ask, "What makes you want to say thank-you to God this morning?" Then gather their words into a prayer. When they feel used to this format, you may say, "Let's say thank-you to God for his goodness to us. Each of you may say something if you wish." You, the teacher, may begin and/or close, "We all have needs with which God can help us. Would you like to pray about these?" The amen said by all reassures each child who prays aloud.

This does not close out the possibilities for spontaneous prayer during the session. Adults do this silently, but children must first learn how. As they look at growing plants, say, "Thank-you, God, for the wonderful way you make flowers grow and children, too." When a child has been crying, pray aloud, "You are near us, God; help ______ to know this and to feel better." When a quarrel has been ended, respond, "Be near us, Lord, and make us friends again."

Some teachers include the offering in the worship service, since this is part of the offering of ourselves to God. It might be more convenient, especially with preschoolers, to have each place the offering in a receptacle as they come to class and say or sing your thanksgiving after one child has brought the offering forward. This may be more a mechanical matter than anything else.

The Bible will always be a part of worship because it is the word through which God speaks. You need use only one or a few verses. The important thing is that children understand the thought. You could read a story, a portion of a psalm, or a brief teaching selection. Sometimes a few words of introduction are helpful, or a brief comment afterwards helps the children remember. Another way to close is by asking the children what they think the Bible reading says. This would lead naturally into prayer together.

Keep the service short. That is important. Again, do not try to make this a substitute for morning worship.

The Life of Prayer

The Sunday School also teaches people how to grow in their own life of devotion. It can teach them how to use the Bible as a way of understanding the meaning of God's word, to pray from it, and to be deepened in prayer because of it. This happens through the sharing of experiences and through the use of the Bible in classes. The encouragement to read the Bible daily at home will frequently come through a Sunday School teacher. It could become a practice by a prayer or Bible study group, particularly when members bring their questions and insights to class.

It might surprise you to know that some people think of prayer only as they participate in Sunday worship. These people still need to learn how to pray alone. The study of the Bible gives the example of people who prayed and what this meant in their lives. Notice this in the Psalms, the Gospels, and the Epistles. To learn about God is to begin to learn how to pray for prayer is first of all the expression of a relationship with God. The example of people who pray is helpful. Sharing insights and experiences is important. The members of a class share a mutual responsibility for Christian growth. How is your class helping?

Children also need a time to talk spontaneously about prayer. When do they pray at home? At meals? At bedtime? When they have done wrong? When they are afraid? When they need help? Learning to pray for others is a development which comes as a child grows old enough to see beyond immediate needs. "Bless mother, dad, and sister" may become habitual words long before the meaning is deepened. Only when one becomes aware of the needs of another can one pray with some insight.

The climax of the work of the Sunday School is seen in the way in which it enables members to grow in the life of prayer, in their personal relationship to God through Christ, and—because of this—in the quality of a Christian life of witness.

Summary

The Sunday School teaches people ways of worship through:

1. The participation of every member in the morning service
2. The study of a reflection upon the hymns, Scripture, and prayer

3. The interaction of parents and children as they attend worship and gather and talk about its meaning at home
4. The forms of worship in Sunday School
5. The help given for individual growth in personal devotion

Index

Index

Iris Cully is one of the country's leading Christian educators. She has taught seminary students, led pastors' retreats, and conducted workshops for Sunday School teachers in cities, suburbs, and rural communities. She is the author of eight books in the field of Christian education and has contributed to other books and magazines. She lives in White River Junction, Vermont, where she and her husband, Kendig Brubaker Cully, edit and publish *The Review of Books and Religion*.